'Roses in D

Memories of Glossopdale and Longdendale

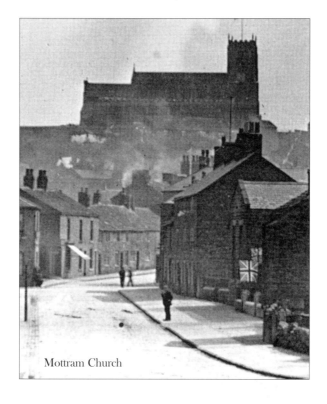

Mottram Church

Mollie Carney

CHURNET VALLEY BOOKS
6 Stanley Street, Leek, Staffordshire. ST13 5HG 01538 399033
www.thebookshopleek.co.uk
© Mollie Carney and Churnet Valley Books 2002
ISBN 1 897949 89 8

Acknowledgments

Mrs Christine Clarkson who undertook the huge task of correcting my manuscript.

Her husband, Michael Clarkson for his Clerical advice

Alex Killeen, my daughter for her support and encouragement.

My son-in-law, Phil Killeen, who most patiently rescued me from my computer more times than I care to remember.

Ms Debbie Harrison who patiently toiled with me for hours and hours whilst writing this book.

Mr Bill Johnson, 25 Ashworth Lane, Mottram in Longdendale SK14 6NT for his generous permission to use many photographs from his book, *Longdendale and Glossopdale*.

Mrs Barbara Wilkins, for memories of Hannah and John Warrington.

The late Francis Dearnley whom I talked to at length about workhouse life.

Mr Frank Dearnley for generously supplying further notes of his late father's account of his life as a Porter at Glossop Workhouse.

Ms Jean Morse for kindly filling in some missing gaps for me.

Ms Sue Essex, Local Studies Dept, Glossop Library, who gave me such generous assistance at all times.

Mrs E. Davies of Glossop Heritage Centre who gave me valuable help.

The Glossop Chronicle, and their valuable archives.

Mr P. B. Robinson, Unicorn Brewery, Frederick Robinson's Ltd. Stockport, who assisted me greatly with their archives of the Junction Inn, Mottram.

Mr Clayton, the licensee of the Junction Inn Mottram who filled in a few gaps.

Ms Alice Lock, Local Studies Librarian, Tameside Local Studies & Archives Unit, who was so very helpful.

C. Wilkins-Jones, *Tameside, an Outline History,* for solving the mystery of 'Riding the Black Lad'.

Sally Ann Cooper (2390) Ordinance Survey.

L. A. Bates, Local Studies Librarian, Derbyshire C. C. County Hall, Matlock.

Glossop Police, who kindly helped me in my detective work.

Mr R. Bullock for permission to use the item on the abolition of stone-breaking, from his book *Salford 1900-1914*.

Sir William Gladstone, for allowing me to quote from one of Catherine Gladstone's letters to her husband.

Lady Jennifer Hill-Wood for permission to use her family photographs.

Thr Dowager Duchess of Norfolk.

The Late Alderman Doyle, my friend, who insisted I read his articles on the Cotton Famine, and so started me off on social history.

Huddersfield Local Studies Library.

Holmfirth Local Studies Library.

Donald Read, *The Age of Urban Democracy England,* Longman.

Helen Perkins, Geography dept, Manchester University.

Kelly's Directories, Cheshire 1906 and Derbyshire 1908.

Mrs Joyce Powell, who generously gave me permission to use photographs in her book *Longdendale in Retrospect,* and gave me information about the Junction and Organ Inns.

The Englishman's Food by J.C. Drummond and Anne Wilbraham.

Mrs Marian Turner and daughter Christine Jones who helped me by providing an update of the ten Wadsworth children.

Mrs Hazel Hall who helped me to sort out the Wadsworth family.

Miss Anne Pacey, Glossop History Society.

CONTENTS

Acknowledgements

Foreword by the Late Duke of Norfolk, Lord Howard of Glossop.

For George

FOREWORD
By The Late Duke of Norfolk, Lord Howard of Glossop

There has been a warm relationship between the Howard family and the town of Glossop for over 300 years.

Present day Glossop still benefits from the benevolence exercised by my family, the Howards, Lords of the Manor, over these many changing years.

During the nineteenth century the Howards were there to see Glossopdale blossom into an incorporated town of much prosperity. They were there to assist when most of Glossopdale suffered severely during the Cotton Famine.

Today our ties with the Town continue. I take a keen interest in being Patron and President of Glossop Heritage Trust. I therefore welcome another book that preserves memories of lives lived in Glossopdale at the beginning of the 20th Century. These memories will soon be lost forever unless they are recorded now.

Norfolk Square in Glossop named in respect for the Norfolk family.

INTRODUCTION

Many years ago when I was a student researching family life of the late Victorian-Edwardian period I became very interested to know just how some of the 'ordinary' people fared. This interest has never left me and I have amassed a wonderful collection of memories throughout my life.

I was interested in the food they ate and the mode of living they adopted to fight against the little life had allotted to their families, without Social Security and a National Health Service to cushion them from the harshness and misfortunes of life.

Most of them would recall in detail the food that their family ate when they were young. I began to listen to some of these 'ordinary' people who were mostly near the end of their lives. I found such rich memories of times long gone and how they had survived life with an unbreakable spirit.

Some of them would write their memories down for me and I have tried to quote them accurately. Some would talk to me whilst I made notes. When I re-read my notes back to them they were only too quick to correct me until I got their reminiscences absolutely correct.

I soon realised that none of the people whose memories I recorded were ordinary. The sheer spirit and ingenuity displayed by some of the mothers who had come to the aid of their families struck me forcefully.

None of my contributors could claim to be famous - not even in the area where they lived out their lives. This is why I feel compelled to allow their lives to be chronicled here, although I have sometimes taken liberties with some of the names to give them a measure of anonymity.

BIBLIOGRAPHY

Manual for Master and Matron, William Golden Lumley Esq. LLM. 2nd edition 1869. Knight and Co, London.

The Englishman's Food, J.C. Druminond and Anne Wilbraham. Jonathan Cape 1964.

Lancashire poets and other Literary Sketches, Thomas Costley 1897.

Glossop During the Cotton Panic, Alderman J D Doyle J.P.

Letters from Catherine Gladstone to her husband William Gladstone during a visit to the distressed regions of the North during the Cotton Famine.

Correspondence with many of the people named in the book. Family papers, letters, documents and photographs.

OS map of Glossop 1899

One

TWENTY YEARS
AT GLOSSOP WORKHOUSE

At the turn of the 20th century the town of Glossop claimed to be the chief seat of the cotton industry in Derbyshire. It was described in one directory as *'a Market town, amidst bleak but picturesque hills'*.

It owed its success mainly to the influence of the Howard family, a branch of that noble family headed by the Duke of Norfolk. In the 1840s George Edward Howard became Lord of the Manor and resided at Glossop Hall.

The Howards had a succession of clever agents who recognised and developed the assets that Glossopvale possessed. It had an abundance of water from the moors which, combined with the fast flowing rivers and streams, gave the area a natural advantage for the successful production of cotton. Another was its geographical position, near the important textile centre of Manchester. It had woollen and paper mills, dyeing, bleaching and print works, as well as iron foundries.

Between 1823 and 1832 plans for a House for the Poor were prepared. The need for a shelter for the poor had been essential from the times when the cotton industry started to attract newcomers to the area to find work, some of them coming from as far afield as Cornwall and Ireland, and, of course, often without relatives at hand in times of need.

In 1832 the old system of Parish Poor Relief was struggling to cope with the changing times, although the relief amounted at that time nationally to a staggering £7 million a year. A national Commission was appointed to overhaul it and resulted in the Poor Law Amendment Act of 1834. There was to be no more outside relief except for the old and the sick, and the relief for the poor was to be in workhouses run by local Union Boards from the parishes. Conditions were to be *"less desirable"* than those of the poorest workers outside the workhouse, the diet was to be basic, and wives and husbands were to be housed separately. The parishes had the powers to raise rates to build and administer the workhouses, and they were run by a board of elected guardians with paid officials.

The new workhouses were soon seen as 'Bastilles' by the poor - they were harsh places, harshly administrated - but the effect was succesful in reducing the burden of the Poor Rates to £4.5 million by 1843.

The new grey stone Workhouse stood isolated from the town by a comfortable two mile walk. It opened in 1832 with Tobias Dickinson as the first Governor and Assistant Overseer at a salary of £45 a year plus full emoluments (food, accommodation and other perks).

Between October 1861 and 1865, the period of the American Civil War, the stock of cotton rapidly diminished and the cotton operatives faced several years of appalling poverty, misery and distress. Local shopkeepers suffered along with the operatives. But with courage and fortitude the people of Glossopvale faced a situation they had not envisaged before.

Lord Edward Howard led the way in trying to alleviate both pride and poverty in the distressed population. Without his support, one doubts that the people of Glossopvale would have survived those long, hungry years. His lead was followed by other local worthies.

The Board of Guardians played their part by borrowing money for public works but they were rigid in the application of the rules, especially the hateful application of the 'Labour Test' for men applying for out-door relief. The tasks set by the Guardians, especially those of stone breaking and oakum picking were bitterly resented. Proud men were forced into tasks such as removing earth and forming a road at the back of the workhouse.

At one stage, the men had to labour for ten hours a day for 1 shilling in cash and 6d in kind. They received no food during their labours and their complaints were not heard. The hated 'Labour Test' had to be endured.

In 1862 Glossop Workhouse was full to overflowing and the Guardians ordered the attics to be floored and plastered to provide more sleeping accommodation. At this time the Assistant Matron was dismissed because there were so many able bodied women in the house competent enough to do her work.

In 1900, the Workhouse buildings stood on the lower slopes of a bleak windswept hill that overlooked Old Glossop and Glossop Town. The long rough track up to the Workhouse widened into smooth green lawns at the Workhouse gate. Formal gardens were laid out in front of the main buildings that housed the Master and Matron - their home and offices and the Boardroom where the Board of Guardians met.

The more recent stone built Infirmary block stood to the left of the main building. Behind this façade was the Workhouse proper that contained the sleeping wards, the kitchen and dining room, the sewing room and the laundry. then there was the work yard, and the workshop and pig sties at the back of the work yard.

It was the Master's job to admit the paupers when old age, infirmity, illness or misfortune forced them to seek shelter within the Workhouse walls, along with young widows with families, deserted wives and orphans.

For mothers with babies born out of wedlock this ordeal could be alarming, for in some workhouses they still retained the custom of issuing the yellow cotton 'disgraceful dress' to be worn by all women with 'bastard children'. Fortunately this custom was fading fast. The mothers of these harshly named 'bastard children' were allocated only very menial tasks, to add to their shame. *The Master and Matron's Manual,* 1869 stated, *"that the Mothers should not be employed upon household work. They should rather be set to pick oakum or some similar tasks."*

All the inmates were without the financial means to live. The workhouse was the very last resort, when all other help failed and the last of the family belongings had gone. They had to resign themselves to the great shame and the indignity of becoming pauper inmates.

The inmate existed upon a routine that was God fearing, orderly, sober and deadly monotonous. The paupers were brought in by the Relieving Officer who had to be a tough character. He worked on a commission basis that formed part of his own income. It satisfied the cost-conscious Guardians that he would leave no stone unturned to extract as much money from the family of the proposed inmate.

In Edwardian days, sons and daughters were financially responsible for their aged parents. Many took their parents into their own homes at first until sickness or poverty befell them as well. 70% of Glossopdale's population worked for 'King Cotton' and his fortunes could fluctuate from year to year. With old people, when admission to the workhouse became a necessity, the Relieving Officer arrived at the home where the elderly parents resided to assess if their children could contribute to their parents upkeep in the Workhouse. It was policy to remove any valuables that had not been sold already before he arrived, but it is not easy to move a piano that was the pride and joy of a family - and the piano had to be sold before any further negotiations could take place.

On admission, new inmates were taken to the 'Receiving Ward' where they were searched. Their clothes were taken away to be fumigated with foul smelling sulphur candles, and they were given a bath in the 'Casual' ward, providing they were not ill.

Their clothes were placed in a labelled sack and stored in the 'Inmates own clothing' store until such time that the inmate would seek their discharge. Any valuables or money were entered in 'The Inmates Property Book'.

There followed an examination by the Medical Officer, Dr Bowden, who gave them their 'Classification'. Within the Workhouse there were seven classes:

1. Men infirm through age or any other cause
2. Able bodied men and youths above the age of fifteen years.
3. Boys over seven and under fifteen years.
4. Women infirm through age or any other cause.
5. Able bodied women and girls above the age of fifteen
6. Girls above the age of seven and under fifteen
7. Children under the age of seven.

Next they were given Workhouse uniform, stamped on the inside, and admitted, either to the 'House', or to the Infirmary, depending upon their state of health.

The Master would see the new inmates on admission and allocate them a job or task. The fit inmates worked daily from 9 am until 4 pm. Refusing to do their job could mean a prosecution. Refusing to do their job on medical grounds meant an examination by the Medical Officer to see if the refusal was justified.

Giving an inmate a job or a task was deliberate. *"The object was to keep the pauper inmates at work so as to lead them to prefer a life of independence rather than to be a charge on the ratepayers."*

When the inmates were classified they were assigned to a ward where similarly classified men and women lived, and they were not encouraged to communicate with the other classes. Wives were separated from their husbands and mothers from their children. Mothers were allowed time to see their children but this was not a right and could not be taken as one.

The Guardians later lessened its strict rules when it came to the elderly. In 1869 *The Poor Law Officers Manual* stated that:

"When any two persons, being husband and wife, both of whom shall be above the age of 60 years, shall be received into any workhouse, such two persons shall not be compelled to live separate and apart from each other in such workhouse. The Guardians shall set apart for the exclusive use of every such couple a sleeping apartment separate from the other paupers."

In 1900, John and Hannah Warrington had been Master and Matron of Glossop Workhouse for several years. They were ideally suited for the job; they were highly respectable, exceedingly thrifty and very conscious of their financial responsibility to the rate-payers.

Before their appointment to the Workhouse, John and Hannah had worked and saved together. John had worked as a carpenter in the joinery department of the Mersey Mill, Hollingworth. They had married young and were very happy together. Sadly Hannah had suffered many miscarriages that she bore stoically and they realised that they faced a future without children. They decided to set out to save the amount of money necessary for the 'bond' they needed to apply for the position of Master and Matron of Glossop Workhouse.

The ' bond' was a tangible sign of their solvency. Less of a problem was presenting the two sureties, necessary for their characters, and a confirmation that they were solvent.

Thrift, not poverty necessitated that they share an egg together to keep living costs down to a minimum. None of the generous table fare kept by her mother Hannah Wadsworth was to be found in the young Warringtons' household before they took over the Workhouse.

Hannah loved her husband dearly and they both shared the same sense of humour. Coming from the large, boisterous Wadsworth family it was pleasant to live a quiet, albeit frugal, life with her beloved John. Hannah had five brothers and four sisters, children of prosperous farmer, Len Wadsworth, who owned several public houses as well as a fleet of horses and waggons. Some of his waggons carried the stone for the building of the Longdendale reservoirs. He carted the stone for Hadfield School and in 1872 he was carting stone to build Hadfield Church. He was also a busy local councillor.

By the time they were appointed to the Workhouse as Master and Matron, John and Hannah had saved a substantial sum of money. John Warrington administered the Workhouse well. He was a kind, just man and always boasted that he had never had to resort to ask for Police support to keep control, unlike many of his colleagues who needed this assistance from time to time.

He applied all the rules that were necessary, and there were many, but as lightly as he could. He allowed inmates to choose their daily tasks as far as it was possible. They were able to approach the Master with their grievances and know that he would listen to them and consider their complaints. The inmates respected and liked him and perhaps this was his secret of keeping control, for their rights were so few. When he encountered any difficulty he referred to his Workhouse bible, the *Manual of the Duties of Poor Law Officers Master and Matron of the Workhouse,* second edition 1869.

In the town John was an equally popular and a highly respected member of the community. Their joint salary was £110 per annum, plus full residential emoluments, which included their food, light and fuel. This came with a furnished residence, a personal maid for the matron and all the domestic help needed to run their household. These advantages made their lives free to pursue their jobs to the full.

As Matron, Hannah found a full rein for expressing her passion for an economical way of living. She was both kind and generous at times but needed the gentle influence of her husband to keep her that way. She thrived on monitoring the cost per year of mustard, salt and pepper, as well as vinegar. If the costs were high it could result in a restriction on the use of these commodities by the inmates. The same applied to the annual cost of snuff and tobacco. This had to be watched carefully for if the cost per year rose too much, a special committee had to be formed to scrutinise these expenses and this could result in a more dramatic reduction of these essential items, as far as the inmates were concerned.

There were diets for all classes of paupers. Food was weighed out as prescribed by the Local Government Board diet sheets displayed upon the dining hall walls. These were large cardboard charts that covered all the diets possible within the Workhouse. The inmates could check by their classification how much food they were entitled to, even to having it weighed out before them. The House Diet was for the inmates, the Children's Diet covered the needs of the children, the Infirmary Diet covered the sick in the Infirmary.

In 1907 the Master of Hayfield Workhouse, at the annual meeting of the Local Government Board expressed amazement that he could not pare his costs down to those of Glossop Workhouse. He did not know how Hannah managed it!

In 1907 the cost of the inmates of Glossop Workhouse upon the local ratepayers was as follows:

114 inmates.
Cost per head for provisions 2s 11d a week
Cost per meal per head, 1½d per meal.
Cost of clothing per head weekly, 3d

This was against the costs of the other Workhouses in the same Union:

Bakewell	4s 2d per head provisions
Chapel-en-le-Frith	3s 10d per head provisions
Hayfield	3s 10d per head provisions
Bakewell	5d per head clothing
Chapel en le Frith	4d per head clothing

The costs at Glossop Workhouse may have been far less than Mr Rowntree quoted, for the cost of labour at the Workhouse was never taken into consideration, nor the fruits of the inmates' labour. This included:

Three pig-sties that were always occupied, the occupants cared for by male inmates.
The cows kept which supplied the inmates with milk and butter.
The poultry also tended by inmates.
All the vegetables grown on the land belonging to the Institution, including potatoes, onions and cabbages, carrots, turnips and swedes.
Apple trees, gooseberry bushes, blackcurrant bushes and a rhubarb patch.

Glossop Workhouse was almost a self-supporting community. The inmates had a choice of job to do and because of this took a pride in the job and usually did it well. Every day when the cows were milked, the porter unlocked the door and took the milk down into the cellar, where it was placed in a large bowl. The cream was skimmed off the milk and placed into a separate bowl. The skimmed milk was used for bread and milk and the rice puddings, and the cream made into butter. This cellar was always kept locked.

The measurement of bread and other prescribed amounts were adhered to most strictly.

The loaf of bread weighed a prescribed amount and the guillotine was set to a certain size, which resulted in the exact weight of bread allowed.

A young niece visiting her Aunt and Uncle temporarily forgot her manners and exclaimed at the sight of the bread being prepared so strictly: *"Oh, Aunt do let them have some more!"* *"Indeed, I cannot possibly, it is not allowed!"* came the shocked reply from Aunt Hannah.

The measuring out of the butter was yet another complex ritual. A senior nurse would take the butter, which was on a board, and lay it on the table. Another board was laid over it which was marked by small holes. It was then pressed and flattened out and a skewer was pierced through the holes in order to mark out the exact quantity of butter allowed to the inmate. It was then cut into pats, lifted by a fork and placed on the weighed slice of bread and passed down the tables until each inmate had their ration of bread and butter. The ritual of meal times could have come straight from *Oliver Twist*.

The inmates assembled in the large glass-roofed dining hall and took their places by the white, scrubbed-topped wooden tables. The men in their blue and white cotton jackets and rough trousers stood on one side of the hall and the assembled women and children, in their blue and white striped cotton dresses, on the other. The women wore navy blue dresses on Sundays.

The Master would walk down the centre of the hall and mount the dais at the end. At breakfast time the inmates would chant *"Good morning Master, Good morning Matron"*.

When there was absolute silence, John would give the signal for Grace to be sung by everyone assembled. This gesture over, the Matron would commence to supervise the handing down of the food along the long wooden tables until all the inmates were served. Grace was sung again when the meal was over and the inmates would file quietly out of the dining hall.

This procedure fascinated the many visiting nephews of Uncle John and Aunt Hannah, although they were not allowed into the dining hall. One curious nephew, Dion, found that if he stood on the house staircase and craned his head through a bannister rail, he could watch it all through a fanlight over the connecting door. This was great fun until one day he could not get his head back through the bannisters! There followed great fuss and excitement until a joiner was summoned to release the inquisitive young man, by sawing the rails either side of his protesting head.

Although Hannah and John had no children of their own to love, there were many nieces and nephews who were always visiting them, with or without their parents. They loved to be at home surrounded by the family children.

Hannah's younger sister, Jane Fisher, with her 3 children, lived in the nearby village of Hadfield where her husband had a painter and decorator's business in Station Road. She often drove over to the Workhouse in their pony and trap. Ada, the baby, was a very noisy infant. The inmates and staff at the Workhouse used to say that they could hear 'Fisher's cat' announcing their arrival from some distance!

The nephews who visited were sometimes allowed to play with the pauper boys. They were always instructed never to get into a fight with them, but if this did happen the nephews were not to hit back at the pauper boys.

The nieces, however, were not allowed to play with the children at all. They were allowed a certain time to play on the swings and see-saws in the pauper childrens' playground though. Hannah's personal maid, Sarah Ellen, escorted the girls back to the house and the pauper children were allowed back in their playground.

Sometimes when a young relative displayed a gift of song they were taken by Hannah into the Women's Day Room where they were lifted up onto the centre table to sing to the old ladies sitting around the room wearing their white lace-trimmed bonnets. A niece with cornflower-blue eyes and flaxen hair, would sweetly render a ballad by Ada Leonora Harris:

Hannah's younger sister, Jane Fisher

'Don't Hurry Little Maiden with your growing,
The youth you squander now you will regret.
Don't bind your tresses up but leave them flowing,'
You're but a blossom on Life's tree as yet
To be young, don't be afraid
Pluck the roses 'ere they fade
'Tis your may time and your playtime,
So don't hurry, little maid.'

or a more tearful ballad by Guy d'Hardelot

'Three Green Bonnets at Church one day,
Dulcie and Daisy and Dorothy May,
Three Green bonnets that nod in a row,
Each bonnet tied with a green ribbon bow
One pair of blue eyes and one pair of grey;
And one pair of brown eyes, that's Dorothy May.

Three little heads at the close of day
Dulcie and Daisy and Dorothy May
Three little heads of clustering curls
Three little beds and three little girls
Brown eyes are sleeping and blue eyes and grey

But angels are peeping at Dorothy May.
Three green bonnets have had their day
Dulcie and Daisy and Dorothy May
Three green bonnets grown old unawares
Hang on three pegs at the foot of the stairs,
Blue eyes are swollen and so are the grey,
For angels have stolen Dear Dorothy May!

There was not a dry eye in the room. Occasionally there would be a less harrowing song to raise the gloom, with a hearty rendering by a visiting nephew of 'To be a farmer's boy' or 'Soldiers of the Queen'.

The niece or nephew was then removed by Sarah Ellen, back to the Master's living quarters for milk and biscuits.

Sarah Ellen, a rather superior inmate, worked as a personal servant to John and Hannah in their Workhouse quarters. The numerous nieces and nephews of John and Hannah who were frequent visitors, called her, 'SirEllin'. She escorted them during their visits to the playground, fed them and gave the younger children baths in the intriguing bathroom in the Master's quarters, before they left for home, dressed in their night clothes and well wrapped up in a cosy blanket. Most of the children were only used to a weekly bath at home, in a long tin bath in front of the kitchen fire.

Mr Frank Dearnley recalls his life as a porter in Glossop Workhouse when Hannah and John Warrington were in charge. He lived and worked in the Workhouse for many years. Like most people new to the workhouse routine, Mr Dearnley was shocked to find himself living with the *"outcasts of society, the poor, the sick, the disabled and the unfortunate."*

Amongst the people he was destined to live among, he thought some of the most unfortunate were the children, and many were the stories he would tell of the patient suffering of the people who later came to be under his care.

Fortunately there were some souls who were quite happy and content and satisfied *"with their lot"*. One of Mr Dearnley's many jobs was to supervise the able-bodied men. In Summertime the time for rising was 6.30 am, in Winter 7 am and the men had a later breakfast but invariably they saved their pint of tea for later. After breakfast the men returned to their day room, until they assembled in the workyard and started off to their jobs.

Mr Frank Dearnley in retirement.

At 9 o'clock Frank Dearnley took round their tea, saved from their breakfast allowance. Between 10 and 11am he took round a tray with pieces of sweet cake, and everyone had a piece. At 12 noon he would ring the bell and the inmates assembled in the dining room. The lunchtime meal would vary from potatoes, swede or cabbage with beef, pork or bacon with rice pudding to follow. Other times it would be a bowl of vegetable soup with suet dumplings.

Most of the food came from the Workhouse farm, and although the variety was poor, the quality of produce was good.

After lunch Frank would ring the bell at 1 o'clock and shout out, *"Now then, hurry up chaps"*, when the men dispersed back to their jobs.

Quite a few of the men were skilled craftsmen and they received a few extras for their services.

Tea was at 5 pm and was a repeat of breakfast.

Saturday lunch was plain - bread, butter and cheese with coffee, and this had to suffice. The reason for this was that, on Saturday, Matron had everything connected with the cooking brought into the dining room where it was all thoroughly cleaned.

Taking all things into consideration Mr Dearnley thought that the inmates did not fare too badly. The food was monotonous but it was wholesome and regular. The relatives would bring in sweets, tobacco and snuff on 'Tuesday Visiting Time', and the men were entitled to 1 oz of tobacco (twist or shag) a week that was distributed on Sunday mornings.

There were religious services every Sunday afternoon conducted by various ministers, for the old and sick. Some workhouse masters had a trick of handing out the weekly perks as the men came out of Church after Morning Service. This was one method to keep church going popular with the male inmates. Those men who did not go to church sometimes did not receive the tobacco.

The older women were given snuff if they so wished. Later boiled sweets were introduced.

The Catholics were allowed a leave pass from 9.45 am to 12.30 to attend All Saints' church. The pass was applied for the day before at the Master's office and the inmate showed the pass to the porter at the Lodge the following day who entered it into the porter's book. If the inmate returned late, the time was entered in red ink in the porter's book so that when the Master initialled the book he would know the culprits!

'Ginger' was an inmate who helped to look after the pigs. He had been in the Workhouse since he was a child and he had what we would now call 'learning difficulties'. When he grew into a young man, Ginger was always trying to escape into the outside world and he was forever being caught and brought back. His strength was such that he would grip on to the wooden bar under the framework of a waggon leaving the Workhouse. Sometimes he would be taken for miles before he was discovered. His strength and endurance were wondered at by the Workhouse staff.

Eventually he was allowed out with a 'Trusty' inmate. The male inmates chopped up old railway sleepers into bundles of firewood to sell to local residents. Ginger, with his 'Trusty', so enjoyed pushing a cart laden with chopped firewood to sell, that he did not stray again.

Hannah with her devoted dog 'Gyp'.

The inmates were given a bath every fortnight, but the opportunity was not always welcomed by everyone. One of the inmates, known as Plunger, was most reluctant.

One day Hannah approached the porter, Frank Dearnley, and said that they had to see if they could persuade Plunger to have a bath. Together they visited him on the ward. The Matron said briskly, *"Come on Plunger, bath night tonight"*, but Plunger flatly refused and a brisk argument followed, at the end of which Plunger said, *"I will have to ask the Lord."* As they all gathered round his bed he closed his eyes, held his hands together in prayer, and solemnly said, *"O Lord have I to have a bath tonight?"*

Matron replied (sotto voce) *"Yes"*. Plunger, in a loud voice, with his strong dialect, retorted, *"Th'art a damn liar; he said nowt ot sort"*.

The men and boys were given a clean shirt and neck tie every week, these numbered so that each person received his own garment back.

A barber named Mr Page from Norfolk Street came regularly to give those who needed it a haircut and shave. There was another barber who came called Higginbottom. He had a shop near the Weighbridge, close to where Glossop Post Office is now. When Frank Dearnley was a boy he used to go to Mr Page's shop for a hair cut. It cost him one penny, but Mr Page always gave him a halfpenny change and said, *"Fer't buy some toffee wi'."*

Hannah took a great interest in Michael who had lived in the Workhouse from being a baby. He did not grow to a normal size and his head appeared to be much larger than his body. Michael also had a large bent nose. He trotted busily around the Workhouse, never parted from his grey tweed floppy hat. He had a short tweedy jacket and his trousers were forever at half mast.

Michael had little respect for authority and would walk up and stare at any visitors, be they members of the Board of Guardians, local clergy or visiting workmen. And Michael could be naughty at times. Early one summer morning he chopped down several large bushes giving welcome shade to the Workhouse kitchen. He was escorted back to his ward and his shoes were removed for two days as punishment.

Michael was indulged by the other inmates as well as Hannah and John. He loved the concerts given by local artistes. He would sit on the end of a wooden form at the back of the hall, where he was placed 'out of harm's way', and invariably embarrass everyone as he sat clumsily upon one end of the form, so the other would tip up and deposit him upon the floor. Up he would scramble, muttering in his own way. He would try another form in exactly the same way, with the same result, until the staff settled him down with them on a safe seat.

Hannah found these concerts 'nerve racking' for the artistes needed appreciation and there were times when they could easily be offended by the audience. Hannah had a beloved dog, Gyp, a greyhound who followed her everywhere, and sneaked into some of the concerts. He had a habit of gradually sliding to the front of the hall under the seats to sit with his mistress. Unfortunately he quickly became bored, but he waited until some well-proportioned soprano began her solo, and as she opened her mouth so did Gyp with a bored howl. The audience had difficulty sorting out one set of vocal cords from the other, and there would be a loud cackling from Michael at the back of the hall. Matron would graciously apologise to the artiste, and have her dog removed before the concert could continue.

At ten years old Alice became an orphan, and until she was adopted she stayed for a year in the Workhouse. She took away with her a hatred of the children's breakfast, memories of having to have her milk allowance in the form of stale bread and hot skimmed milk, called 'Pobs', and the only breakfast allowed. That some of the children disliked this dish made no difference.

Alice found little to praise, remembering long dull days and jeers from the village children when she walked in a crocodile to the school 'outside' of the Workhouse, down in the village of Old Glossop - the workhouse children were easy to distinguish because of their workhouse clothing.

Here the Duke of Norfolk School and the Glossop Parish church stood side by side. The church was rumoured to be 'High'. In those days the line was sharply drawn between the English Church and Rome, and if the church was 'High', then most folk thought the Vicar was half way to Rome. All Saints Catholic Church and school were a couple of hundred yards away.

There was a playground at the Workhouse with swings for the children to use when they returned from school. There were some toys donated by local dignitaries as well as books for those children *'who expressed a desire for them'*.

Fresh fruit like oranges were rarely given and sweets were only seen at 'treats'. Dinner time meals varied, sometimes it was stew or broth with dumplings. The broth was rather tasteless and watery. Rice pudding seems to have been the standard pudding - not popular with the inmates of course, and made from skimmed milk.

Tea was the last meal of the day and this was always bread and butter and tea. There was no supper and bed time was very early.

The food was dull and the monotonous regularity must have made it appear even duller to a child of ten. She also remembers the grumbles of the adult inmates. The children had to go into the kitchen for their meal at dinner time where the cook would serve them their food. At breakfast and teatime the children had their food in the dining room along with the other inmates under the watchful eye of the Master and Matron. Alice says as a result of the workhouse, when she grew up she was always satisfied with small amounts of food.

She finally went into service and became an excellent servant. She was lucky to be adopted so soon into a good home - this was always the orphan child's hope, that they would be adopted. If they were not fortunate enough to be adopted by families 'outside', the children had to wait patiently until they were old enough to be sent out into the world to fend for themselves. The girls were taught housework and many of them went into domestic service. The women's and girls' health and cleanliness were supervised by the Matron and Assistant Matron, Miss Finder. The girls were supplied with a wardrobe of clothes when they left for domestic service: 2 print dresses; 1 navy serge dress; 1 brown hat; 1 brown coat; 2 chemises; 2 pairs of drawers; 2 pairs of stockings; 2 flannel petticoats; 1 pair of boots; 1 pair of shoes; 6 handkerchiefs; 1 comb and brush; 4 new aprons, all good; 2 pairs of gloves; 1 toothbrush.

A member of the Board of Guardians was quoted: *"A Countess or a Duchess could not have had a much better outfit."* He went on, *"A large number of the Public, when they take the children into their service, sneer at them because they have come from the Workhouse.*

This was wrong. People should not sneer but encourage them to work and to conduct themselves properly. This would be a blessing to the children and a benefit to the community at large."

The boys from the Workhouse were found jobs or were apprenticed. One boy raised in Glossop Workhouse became a Mayor of Glossop and a most respected Alderman.

On Liberty Day each month, when the inmates were allowed out for the day to seek work, they were issued with a clean shirt, tie and socks, a suit of clothes, complete with a muffler if it was cold. The women changed out of their blue and white striped cotton dresses and donned 'individual' clothes to visit relations or search for work.

At Glossop, few inmates failed to return at the allotted time and of the few who did occasionally stray, John dealt with them leniently. One man who had stayed out for three nights turned up the fourth night with the Casuals who were waiting to be admitted. The porter Mr Dearnley, reported the man's presence to the Master who suggested the man be given a bath and brought before him.

"I'll have a word with him" said Mr Warrington [the Master].

The culprit was wearing an old worn suit and down at heel boots.

"Where are the good set of clothes and boots we sent you out in," he asked. *"What happened to them?"*

In all probability the man had bartered his good clothes and boots for old ones in order to get some money to spend on the 'Demon drink', but after listening to a caution and a warning of what would happen to him if this occurred again the culprit replied, *"Oh Mester Warrington, Let bygones bi' bygones, a' ll non do it agen."*

The Master turned to Mr Dearnley the Porter; he smiled and said, *"Take him away and give him some food, fresh clothes and let him come back inside again".* Had the rules been applied it would have hurt the Master more than the inmate concerned, Mr Dearnley thought. At another Manchester Workhouse the inmates were not so fortunate. Any man who failed to report back after his liberty day was immediately reported to the Police and when caught was charged with stealing Workhouse property - the clothes that he was wearing.

Despite a cobweb of rules and regulations, John and Hannah tried their utmost to make life bearable for the inmates in their care.

On Bonfire Night there was always a Bonfire near the old quarry at the back of the building. Hannah provided 'parkin' and treacle toffee. Most of her guests and relatives brought fireworks. On one particular Bonfire Night, Hannah's sister-in-law, Sarah, arrived with her son Jack. Sarah could always be depended upon to liven up the proceedings. Jack wandered off on his own and decided to climb up on one of the pig sty walls to get a better view of the celebrations. In his excitement he slipped, lost his balance and fell backwards into the pig manure. Sarah saw the incident from a distance and laughed, not recognising the pathetic sight as her son. She exclaimed, *"That boy is in for a hiding when he gets home tonight".* At the end of the evening, when everyone was preparing to leave, a pungent smell emerged from the shadows. It was Jack. Sarah was not at all amused. Wrapping him in an old blanket, 'SirEllin' retreated from Jack as soon as possible; the stench was overwhelming. Sarah and Jack had to drive the three miles home to Hollingworth in their pony and trap, and although the crisp, moorland air helped, she did not enjoy the drive! Only when Jack's offending clothes were burning in the yard and he was soaking in the tin bath before the fire, did Sarah's famous sense of humour return - she decided he had been punished enough.

Early in December the Assistant Matron, Miss Finder aided by Mr Dearnley would start to make the Christmas puddings for the festive season. Some of the churches sent toys and books, papers and sweets. The dining room was decorated with holly and flags and bunting by the inmates, and local entertainers like the 'Mississippi Minstrel Troupe' were invited to entertain. Frank Dearnley says: *"To see these people enjoying themselves after partaking of Festive fare was indeed something to remember. No effort was spared by those concerned to make these poor people happy on this special occasion."*

Christmas day could be relied upon to provide them with a feast. It was given space in the local *Glossop Chronicle*:

December 1900. Glossop Workhouse.

"At 12.30 the Inmates assembled in the Dining hall and after Grace had been said,the dinner was promptly served and they were soon enjoying the admirably cooked viands and testing the quality of the roast beef, roast pork, boiled mutton, vegetables, puddings and pies.

Dinner over, the inmates sang grace and thanked with acclamation the Guardians for giving the treat.

Oranges, apples, sweets and tobacco were distributed and the Inmates then retired to spend the day in pleasant manner.

A good tea was subsequently served."

Depending on the generosity of the Master, the House rules were relaxed on Christmas Day. Mothers received their children and talked with their husbands for a period during the afternoon. Some of the Guardians made a tour of the institution and spoke to selected inmates exchanging seasonal greetings, even shaking hands with those whose age commanded a show of respect.

But the Guardians and other distinguished guests soon retired to the comfortable quarters of the Master and Matron to refresh themselves before returning, feeling suitably virtuous, to the normality of their prosperous households.

At tea time the inmates emerged from their Day rooms into the decorated dining hall to a tea of bread and butter and jam followed by a piece of currant cake and the usual pint of tea.

The feasting over it was back to their Day rooms. In these sparsely furnished rooms the Windsor chairs formed a half-circle around the hearth where a coal fire burned. The floor was bare apart from a square of coconut-matting placed before the hearth. The only other furniture in the room was a table which on high days and holidays held papers and books donated by local worthies. A lone gas jet spluttered in a light in the centre of the room which, aided by the firelight, warned off the bleak night that stared through the curtainless windows. Here the inmates sat until the bell rang at eight o'clock for bed and lights out.

Boxing Day dawned without hope, for the routine was as undistinguished as any other day in the pauper inmates' existence.

The staff had their own Christmas 'do', but Frank Dearnley says: *"I am pleased to say that as far as the food and enjoyment was concerned it was in no way superior to that previously enjoyed by the inmates."* The staff enjoyed dancing and singing. There was 'An Arab's Farewell to his Steed' sung by John Warrington. Mr Waterhouse, Chairman of the Board of Guardians and Mr Levy James, the Relieving Officer, sang 'Jane, my pretty Jane'. Mr Dearnley waltzed around the room with Mrs Hannah Warrington, the Matron, and everyone enjoyed dancing the Roger de Coverley.

From time to time there were other ' treats' provided for the inmates and these occasions were reported in the *Glossop Chronicle*. Fortunately - unfortunately for the inmates - Coronations were few and far between. For the Coronation of King Edward VII, the inmates received two treats.
The Glossop Chronicle tells us;

"At noon yesterday, the inmates of the Glossop Union Workhouse were entertained to a substantial dinner by the members of the Board of Guardians:

Menu
Roast Mutton and vegetables
Roast Beef and Boiled Mutton Puddings
Tarts, fruit pies,
Beer, or coffee, as the inmates desired.

After the Dinner tobacco and oranges were distributed.
The Dining Hall in which the repast was served was decorated with shields and flags and presented an artistic appearance. The festivity proved a red letter day in the monotonous lives of the poor people."

and:

"Today Councillor and Mrs Herbert Partington will provide a capital repast for the inmates, the good things including a sandwich tea, ham, tongue, fancy bread, oranges, sweets and tobacco.
An entertainment provided by Mr Walter Braddock's giant gramophone will give selections. In the evening the inmates will be given a 'substantial supper'. Councillor Herbert and Mrs Partington deserve all praise for letting in a ray of sunshine into the otherwise dark lives of those unfortunate people."

Both the Partingtons were on the Board of Guardians, Mrs Partington for many years, while her husband, Herbert, was a member for several years before his death in 1916.

The inmates of the Workhouse Infirmary were not forgotten by the 'outside'. At a Harvest Festival Thanksgiving in 1903, one of the local clergy wrote in his diary:

"Harvest Thanksgiving. The children came up to the Chancel and put their offerings into two clothes baskets. The one for perishable goods was filled with offerings, 50 eggs, biscuits and a jelly, grapes, apples, pears and vegetables. In the other basket many preserves were placed. The 15 pots of jam I will take them up to the Workhouse Infirmary throughout the year to come."

Hannah Warrington's eldest brother Tim Wadsworth died from a heart attack at 44 years of age. His prosperous hay and straw business in Hadfield soon deteriorated in the hands of the manager left in charge. Within 2 years Maria his widow and daughter Ellen were destitute. Everything including their family house had to be sold to cover the debts incurred by the manager, and Hannah's youngest brother Arthur Wadsworth, who owned the Junction Inn in Mottram, took both Maria and Ellen into his home.

A family conference was held to discuss what was to become of the mother and daughter who had managed to keep their misfortunes secret until it was too late for anyone to intervene. Maria, took a post as housekeeper to an eminent clergyman and his wife in East Retford in distant Nottinghamshire. Fortunately she had been well-trained domestically and had run her own household to perfection. She had not worked before her marriage to Tim but stayed home to help her mother in the home.

It was decided that Ellen, her daughter, should live with her Aunt Hannah and Uncle John and work in the Workhouse Infirmary until she was old enough to train for nursing, perhaps somewhere nearer to her mother.

Poor Ellen reacted with shock when she first went to work in the Workhouse Infirmary. She understood that there were rules and regulations to be observed all of the time and that these sometimes interfered with kindness and compassion; she was aware that the inmates were paid for by the generosity of the Board of Guardians, in turn funded by the local ratepayers; but Ellen wrote many sad letters to her gentle mother about the overbearing rules.

Selected female inmates assisted the nurses. They cleaned the wards and acted as messengers between the wards. Ellen was greatly distressed to see wedding rings removed from the patients who died. She knew that every few months a man came and bought them in bulk. The money received was put into a ' Burial Account' and used to pay for Pauper funerals. There was little dignity in dying. When all attempts failed to trace a relative who could pay for the burial, the Workhouse had to foot the bill. There was an arrangement with one of the local undertakers to provide cut price burials. All that was provided was a cheap wooden coffin and a workhouse was never far away from a cemetery. At Glossop it was merely a matter of loading the coffin onto a handcart and commandeering two strong male inmates to push it up the steep incline outside the Workhouse and left along Cemetery Road to the hill top cemetery. Hopefully a willing clergyman would be waiting at the common grave to say a few words over the coffin before it was interred.

Early in the 20th Century, a voice in the wilderness spoke out. A spokesman in the medical journal, *The Lancet*, said:

"The days of penal servitude for the sick and aged may come to an end as soon as the Guardians have grasped the idea that old age and sickness are not criminal".

John & Hannah Warrington at the start of their career

The Wadsworth boys. Tim, Tom, George, Len and Arthur. Len Ford is on Arthur's knee.

Some of the Wadsworth brood. Hannah stands behind her mother with her hand on Elizabeth's shoulder.
Arthur is standing the other side with his hand on the shoulder of eldest sister Mary. Jane is on her mother's lap.

Maria Wadsworth, widow of Tim Wadsworth

Ellen Wadsworth (left) niece of John and Hannah. She worked in the Infirmary until she left to study nursing. Ellen is with her cousin Jane Wadsworth.

Glossop Hall home of Lord Edward Howard.

Inside a tramp's cell in the workhouse.

Workhouse Infirmary Glossop.

Two
CASUALS IN THE WORKHOUSE

The Master has the beef
The Porter has the bones
The Inmates get the gravy
The Tramps get the stones.

Verse written on the Tramp Ward wall at Glossop Workhouse.

This chapter is based on the memories of the late Mr Francis Dearnley, born in September 1888 in a small cottage in Old Glossop. He was the middle child of seven children. He was the Porter when John & Hannah Warrington were Master and Matron in the early 1900s. I talked to Mr Dearnley in the late 1960s Also, his son has most generously allowed me to see his father's book of memories.

How did this section of the people fare in Edwardian times? Did the doctrines of Samuel Smiles linger and what was the public attitude to the men who had opted out of the effort to keep Britain ruling the world industrially and in military might?

Tramps using the Workhouse Casual Wards were not always hungry men. It was not unusual for the Porter to find the breakfast bread untouched in the cell when the man had departed, for he had probably only wanted a roof over his head for the night. The farms and houses of the surrounding countryside rarely refused food to a tramp. The man was comparatively well fed.

In the country there was pure air to breathe and fine hedges to shelter beneath. When the night air turned cold they took shelter for the night lying behind a sleeping cow in a field, for here was a warm spot and a chance of a nourishing breakfast drink all in one!

During the long summer days the hours would be wiled away. A cottage or a farm could always be relied upon for a crust or two and a gentleman's house would nearly always provide scraps. If the effort was made to ensnare a rabbit, a royal feast was to be had around a fire in the quiet of the evening.

If the tramp was armed with a 'Tramp map' he was known as a 'Moucher'. The map gave him an idea of how to organise his wanderings. The map would say *'Don't go in that direction, very poor, give nothing;* also *'Silence is best with these people. Say as little as you can.'* In another neighbourhood the map would indicate, *'Mind this way; you may get into prison if you don't.'*

When the days became shorter and the evenings were cold and dark, the tramps would join a circuit of workhouses while the snow and winds took over their happy hunting grounds. The bleak moorland and the grim majesty of the Pennines were too much for the tramps in winter, no matter how well they were organised with their maps.

Gypsies had a similar idea. They used 'markers', patterns of twigs and branches, usually outside churches or the larger houses in the district. It was not as reliable as the Tramp maps, for when local children discovered the markers they took great delight in altering them.

One circuit of workhouses was Hayfield to Glossop, from Glossop to Penistone, then back to Hayfield. This moving about was a necessity because of the Local Government Board

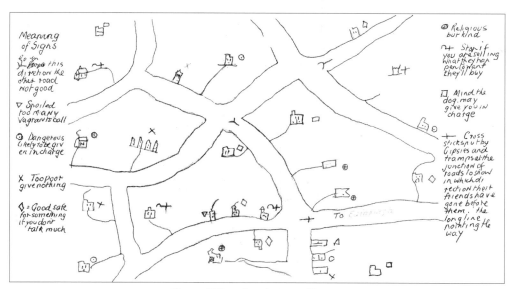

Copy of Chart found upon a Tramp

rule that a tramp may not sleep for more than one night in any one tramp ward ('known to tramps as the 'Spike', 'Grubber' or even 'Clink House Park').

The men, women and children who used the Tramp Wards never came into contact with the Workhouse inmates, mainly to prevent the introduction of infection and contagious diseases into the Workhouse proper.

As the light began to fade in the late afternoon the tramps would appear. They would wend their way to the Workhouse in ones and twos, the few coppers that they possessed securely hidden a mile or so back in a place known only to themselves. Up the side drive they would walk for they were never allowed to use the main drive, and into the welcoming warmth of the Porter's lodge. The Porter, Frank Dearnley, was responsible for the Tramp Wards. He would be at the lodge from 4 until 6 pm. The tramps would sit there until the last man arrived at 6 pm. Armed with his large ledger 'For Vagrants' Frank led the way to a large room on the ground floor, with forms to sit upon, and a solitary desk where he sat to officially register the men into the Tramp or Vagrant wards.

The man nearest the Porter stood up, arms outstretched, to be searched for tobacco, matches and money. If the tramp had fourpence he was refused a bed and directed away to the town's lodging houses. Needless to say there were few men found to have four pence upon them, they were much too cute for that, those knights of the road!

Matches were a real danger to the men in the cells, hence the search for tobacco and matches. If a man was allowed in his cell with matches he may be tempted to light up his pipe - and the cells were locked on the outside! Their 'baccy', matches and pipes were taken away from them and tied up in a cloth along with other personal objects which were listed and put into labelled boxes to be locked away in a spacious iron cupboard on the Tramp ward.

There was another large room on the left that contained a big gas oven that was used to stove their clothes by lighting sulphur candles. It was not the best of odours and it lingered upon the clothes when they were returned to the 'Casuals' the following morning. In the room was a coke fired boiler used for water and heating and this helped to dry their clothes as well.

After the search, the vagrants were registered in the book: Name; where they had come from, and where they were heading for. They were reminded that if they stayed more than one night a week at any one Casual Ward, then the Local Government Board was entitled to detain them for four days - and work them.

The only night that a bath was compulsory was Friday night and as several men would kick against it, they were supervised by a tough-looking 'Tramp Major', a specially chosen, sturdy inmate whose job was to see that the men used the bath there for that purpose.

At this stage the Tramp Major escorted the men to their 'cell' in the Tramp ward, the tramps suitably dressed in visibly stamped workhouse night shirts .

The Casual Ward consisted of several small, narrow cells. Each cell had a bare iron bedstead, minus mattress, covered with three planks of wood. Upon the planks were folded three rough woollen blankets. This was another discouragement to the professional tramp by depriving him of the free and unrestrained comradeship that often took place in the older open Casual wards. To isolate a man and lock him in for the night would discourage all but the honest destitute wayfarer and so ease the financial burden upon the ratepayers.

The women and children's compartments were at the extreme end of the male Tramp Ward, divided from it by a stoutly locked door. In each compartment was the same iron bedstead covered by wooden planks with three blankets placed upon the wooden planks.

All the Casual Ward cells were bolted from the outside. In every cell or compartment there was a bell that would ring in Frank Dearnley's room. No matter what time it was, if a bell rang Frank was obliged to get out of bed to go and see what was wrong in that particular cell. Sometimes the tramp was taken ill and it was Frank's job to inform the Master and Charge nurse so that the sick person could receive medical aid.

Cells in Workhouse Tramp Wards

The casuals were fed in their cells:

Supper: 8 ounces bread. One pint hot or cold water (according to preference)

Breakfast 6.30am Summer. 7am Winter. 8 ounces bread 1 pint hot or cold water.

After their breakfast their clothes were returned to them. The authorities demanded that in return for food and lodging afforded to the tramps, they performed the following tasks:

Males: The breaking of stones $1^{1}/2$ to 3 cwt. according to the hardness of the stone. Or $1^{1}/2$ pounds of oakum to pick.

Females were to be given half a pound of oakum to pick.

Oakum is the material produced by picking asunder the strands of old thick and tarred, hempen ropes discarded by naval vessels in shipyards and used for 'caulking' the seams between the planks of vessels to prevent leaking. The picked oakum from workhouses and prisons was dispatched to the nearest shipyard (Liverpool) to be used again.

Glossop Workhouse had a large slab of stone with a small, scooped out hollow of a few inches at one end. The slab was kept in the work yard of the Workhouse and used as a guide for the tramps to the size of stone required when breaking stones. The stones were used as a base for road building.

Tasks in the work yard were mostly breaking stones until 10am. Once the task was completed to the satisfaction of one of the Workhouse staff the tramps were reissued with the rest of their possessions and allowed to go.

Sometimes, after the tramps had departed, Frank Dearnley would find a memento or two written on the wall of the Tramp Ward:

> "I am but a poor old tramp locked in a workhouse cell,
> I've been worked hard and soon will be in hell,
> But when I get to those fiery gates with a thought to quench my thirst,
> The devil will say, you go away, I want this porter first."

> "Of all the trades in London
> The beggar's is the best,
> For when a man is weary
> He can sit him down and rest".

Frank Dearnley thought that people who could write these lines would not be so stupid as to leave their money in a stone wall near the Workhouse. It was a well known story amongst the local children, who regularly searched the dry stone wall leading up to the Workhouse in case the story was true. The tramps were too cute for this and it was generally believed that the tramps made a show of putting the money in the wall by disturbing the odd stone or two, when he had already hidden it somewhere else.

Occasionally a whole family would visit the Tramp Ward. The mother and children were put together to sleep. The mother would soon have a pot of tea or a mug of cocoa instead of the normal water and as much bread as she could eat. The children would have bowls of bread and skimmed milk instead of bread and water. The following morning they would have the same food and were allowed to go as soon as possible. Most workhouses took pity on a woman with a child. Regulations asserted themselves however and they would still be locked into a cell for the night to sleep as best they could. The following morning they were fed and the woman was expected to pick half a pound of oakum before they went upon their way. Frank says, *"I have seen a mother clutching the hand of a little child on the stone steps of the Tramp Ward. I have looked into the eyes of the bewildered child as it walked along the corridor to a bed of boards and a covering of rugs. God forbid that I ever see such a sight again."*

He also says: *"Many are the recollections I have of tragic incidents that took place between those walls during the times I was employed there. Some tasks I had to fulfil were accompanied with considerable danger and on more than one occasion I was fortunate to get away with a whole skin."*

The only other body who could use the casual wards after hours for vagrants were the local police force. A key was kept at the Police Station and they could bring a needy tramp for the night if he had been found wandering in the town and was without money for a bed.

Conditions did vary and not all were as accommodating as Glossop Workhouse. In one Manchester district, the inmates in the Tramp Ward had to sit in their cell to do their 'Task'. The single storey Tramp Ward building faced into the workhouse yard, and the weighed amount of stone (usually 1cwt) was placed in a wheelbarrow and wheeled into the man's cell. It was then tipped in front of an iron grill and the man had to break up the stones small enough to pass through the iron grill which fell into the yard. When his Task was finished the tramp was obliged to brush out the cell to the porter's satisfaction before he was allowed to leave.

On the other hand in Salford, the question of keeping the increasing numbers of male vagrants was discussed at a public lecture, *Our laws in relation to Beggars and Tramps* in 1900. One of the Guardians said:

"We should not starve the tramps under our control. They should have a night's lodging and as much food as will satisfy them the next day. If they prefer tea and gruel, I don't see why they should not have it. I think there should be no limit with regard to the bread supplied to tramps when in Casual wards".

Let us hope that the gentleman's hopes were realised but for sure it was only after many battles with other members of his Board of Guardians. In April 1911, a motion stating that stonebreaking by workhouse inmates was considered by a minority of the Board of Guardians as *'Cruel, worse than useless, degrading and unprofitable'* was rejected at a meeting of the Salford Guardians by 15 votes to 3.

In the House of Commons in May, 1911, Mr Will Thorne, Labour, asked the President of the Local Government Board if he was aware that in the past few days a lady member of the Salford Union Guardians had spent two hours stone-breaking with a view to testing whether such work was suitable for union inmates. Before completing the work she went to a meeting of the Guardians and asked for the abolition of stonebreaking as a labour test. In view of the feeling existing against this task, the President of the Local Government Board, Mr Burns, was asked to be prepared to advise the Guardians that it be abolished. Mr Burns agreed that stonebreaking was not an ideal task, *'but it was a common form of employment for labourers and although he wouldn't press for its adoption as a task by the Board of Guardians, he would hesitate to prohibit it.'*

The Churching of the Mayor Ceremony.
John Warrington in civic procession with James Malkin, Mayor. John is centre left.

Old Glossop Cross with the Parish Church in the background.

Three
THE SOCIAL LIFE
OF THE MASTER AND MATRON

Glossop was a prosperous town because of the cotton mills which arrived in the early 19th Century. Glossopvale was fortunate to have the benign presence of the Howard family as the old Lords of the Manor. The Howards built the Town Hall and Market Hall, and later they added Norfolk Square which gave a pleasant centre to the town. Through their foresight, a technical school was built in 1899.

Gradually other benefactors added other useful facilities to the town. This may have been a result of a desire to pay something back to the town and the workforce that had helped them make their fortunes by their honest labour. Perhaps there was a suspicion amongst the workforce that it was a more public way to demonstrate their generosity than giving their workers a good living wage in the first place! Such public generosity was another way of gaining recognition and reward.

Samuel Wood and his son Samuel.

John Wood came to the town in 1819 and eventually owned the town's largest cotton mills. He married a Miss Hill from Liverpool and built Whitfield House.

John Wood was a generous benefactor and was well loved in the town, especially in Whitfield. On his death his sons, Samuel, Daniel and John, took over the mills.

Daniel Wood later built the larger family home of Moorfield House where he lived with his brother Samuel and Samuel's formidable wife, Anne Kershaw Wood.

As the Wood family's gift to the people of Glossop on the occasion of Queen Victoria's Golden Jubilee, Mrs Kershaw Wood obtained from Baron Howard 12 acres of land off the beginning of Dinting Road. At her personal expense of £6,000 she brought landscape gardeners from London to create a magnificent 12 acre park. Her husband and his brother Daniel bore the cost of building a Cottage Hospital at the top of the park, forever known as 'Wood's Hospital' and a large public swimming baths near the entrance of the park.

At first the park was named Victoria Park but later it became Howard Park in deference to Baron Howard of Glossop who gave the land.

Samuel and Daniel Wood both died in 1888 and Anne had a monument erected at the park entrance as a memorial to them and the town's conection with the cotton industry. In 1912 the family adopted the name of Hill Wood and from 1910 to 1929, Anne's son, Sir Samuel Hill Wood, was MP for the High Peak

John and Hannah Warrington were well established socially in the town of Glossop. John took an active part in the town affairs, and a great interest in the welfare of the town. He was generous in his support of deserving causes like the Relief of Local Distress Committee. The couple had a strong religious faith and for

Mrs Anne Kershaw-Wood.

many years John was People's Warden at Glossop Parish Church. He took Hannah along to the Parish Church after their appointment to the Workhouse. Hannah's own church was Christ Church, Tintwistle.

John took an active part in the restoration at the Parish Church. He gave his time and put his practical abilities at the disposal of those connected with the restoration work. Together John and Hannah worked tirelessly to raise money, and when the restoration was completed they were thrilled and delighted.

They also took a keen interest in the Church School built in the shadow of the church, for they had a great affection for children.

Although it was not the usual policy for masters of workhouses to openly declare their politics, John was an active member of Glossop Conservative Party. Glossop was a stronghold for the Liberal party because many local industrialists and their workers were supporters. But John's sincere and pleasant manner made him a popular and respected member of the community.

John was the proud owner of a black umbrella with an ivory handle and a thick gold tip. It had a small gold band around the top of the stick engraved with his name. It simply stated, "John Warrington of Glossop".

Moorfield, the Glossop home of the Hill Wood family.

Howard Park from the Lake. Wood's Hospital is in the background.

Their quarters at the Workhouse were spacious and comfortably furnished for Hannah had impeccable taste. Combined with an abundance of domestic help that included several inmates who had been in domestic service, the couple were able to live in a gracious manner. Throughout the years some of their accumulated savings were invested in fine linen and silver as well as delicate and beautiful china. Many of the female inmates were skilled craftswomen whose crochet work embellished much of Hannah's household and bed linen.

John bought his wife some handsome jewellery to go with her tasteful clothes, so that suitably dressed and bejewelled she graced his table when they entertained guests. When they entertained Hannah always consulted Polly, her sister-in-law, an excellent cook and hostess. When a formal dinner party was held, Polly would drive over from the Junction Inn at Mottram where she assisted her husband Arthur in running the Inn. She would prepare the more sophisticated dishes and supervise the kitchen - Hannah could smile and relax with her guests and know that all was well once Polly was in charge.

Hannah and John's friends tended to be connected with their work. William J. Bowden was Medical Officer for No.1 District of the Union until 1909. He became a firm friend and, with his wife Annie, often dined with them. They had many friends among the Board of Guardians, James Malkin, a prosperous corn merchant, was a past Chairman of the Board of Guardians. Mr Thomas Swindells Bowden was Clerk and Registrar. His son, the Dr William just mentioned, was known affectionately amongst family and friends as Willie.

John was also a Mason and held high office - Provincial Grand Treasurer in the Province of Derbyshire - so there were many friends amongst his fellow Masons. He was in the Devonshire Lodge of Freemasons of Glossop with William Bowden, James Malkin and Herbert Partington.

Mrs Mary Partington had been for many years on the Board of Guardians and her husband, Herbert, eventually joined her as Chairman. They were on good terms with John and his wife and met socially. James and Clara Malkin often invited John and Hannah to supper parties held at their home, Brook House, on Sheffield Road.

These friends had another connection; they were all devout churchgoers at Glossop Parish church. The Malkins' children, Dorothy and Robert, attended the same private school in Glossop as Hannah's niece, Jane Wadsworth. Jane and Dorothy became bosom friends throughout their lives.

The Malkins did a lot of entertaining. They had one resident maid but outside help was always there for special occasions. Clara Malkin did most of the day-to-day cooking - she was a good cook who enjoyed cooking for her family, but when large numbers were entertained she would call in one of the smart caterers.

Later the Malkins moved to Moorside, a large and elegant old house with seven bedrooms. The house stood way up above Old Glossop and overlooked the front of the Workhouse and the wild, majestic hills beyond. They acquired a second resident maid until Dorothy, their daughter, could give a hand in running the house. Middle class daughters rarely went out to work at this time.

Clara Malkin gave 'at homes' once a month when she would prepare thin bread and butter, white and brown scones, and delicate small cakes. This was brought into the drawing room by a maid while Clara sat and poured tea for her friends who called. Sometimes there

James Malkin

Clara Malkin

Taking afternoon tea at Beechwood, North Road, Glossop.

might be only one caller, at other times six. As her guests left they would leave their cards on a small silver tray in the hall with their 'at home' days printed on them so Clara could return the calls.

Hannah rarely attended these for she was usually busy and the Workhouse was no place to have 'at homes'. Hannah was close to her brother Arthur Wadsworth and his wife Polly, and to her younger sister, Jane, known in the family as 'Lady Jane'.

Hannah and John bought a plot of land at the bottom of Hadfield Road opposite the Vicarage in Hadfield. They built a modest stone house with a staff cottage attached for a housekeeper and gardener. They called their new home Beech House and the date under the eaves was 1890. They would retreat to the house in their off duty hours and they planned to live there in their retirement.

For several years they ventured abroad with friends, and enjoyed visits to France and Italy. Other years they visited Ireland and the Isle of Man. They both had the same sense of humour - Hannah made John laugh out loud by recounting the 'goings on' in the town of the socially ambitious middle class.

The Mayoral Banquet and Ball in 1907 was given by Herbert Partington, the son of a wealthy industrialist, on his first election to Mayor, an office he would hold four more times. His father, Captain Edward Partington, came to Glossop in 1873 at the age of 27 and bought a paper mill at Turn Lee. This was the beginning of the worldwide Kellner Partington Paper and Pulp Company. Both his sons, Oswald and Herbert, lived locally. The Mayoral Banquet and Ball was the social event of the year in Glossopdale, and it was recalled for many years. *The Glossop Chronicle* reported:

> "The Victoria Hall and Library was transformed by an interior decorator from London, a Mr. Houghton, and his assistants for this important event.
>
> As the guests entered they found the principal staircase lined with purple carpet and the walls adorned with garlands of roses and festoons of evergreen, while the latter was very naturally entwined round the trellis work which led from the kerbstone to the hall steps and was dotted here and there by choice blooms.
>
> The Ballroom walls were draped in satins of green, old rose and white. In the centre of the Ballroom was a canopy draped in old rose and from the corners were suspended baskets of roses and trailing evergreens.
>
> Other rooms were artistically adorned with baskets of roses and garlands of roses and carried through the colours of gold, cream and green.
>
> The Supper Room was a rich feast of colour, and the Reading Room was set apart for the Gentlemen's Smoke Room.
>
> At every turn, tall majestic palms and lovely foliage plants were displayed to the view and provided a cooling effect in each room."

Amongst the glittering list of guests that appeared in the paper, between members of the Board of Guardians and the Borough Treasurer and Town Clerk, we find the names of Hannah and John Warrington.

How splendid they must have looked as they circled the Ballroom floor to the waltz, *Count of Luxembourg*. The Banquet was held in a room which had been transformed for the evening. Countless silver candlesticks adorned the tables and other points of vantage, with

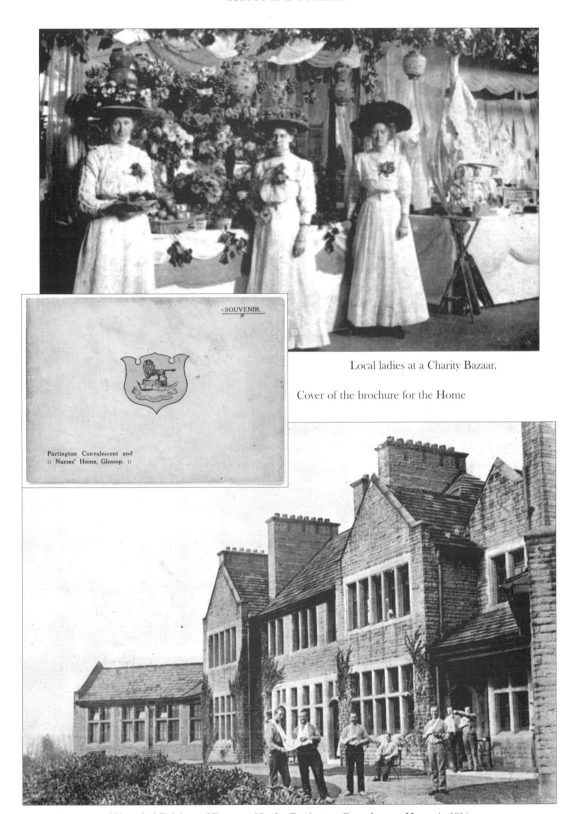

Local ladies at a Charity Bazaar.

Cover of the brochure for the Home

Wounded Belgian soldiers outside the Partington Convalescent Home in 1914.

rich and vari-coloured shades which cast a soft glow over the diners. On the table were pink tulips and white lilies, with foliage of brilliant green, a magnificent floral adornment.

The menu was:

Consommé Printanière
Saumon à la Mayonnaise
Salade d'homard
Dinde farcie au Suprême
Dindon chaudfroid
Poulard à l'Elysée
Jambon braisé de York
Terrine de Gibier
Langue écarlate
Boeuf pressé au Chasseur
Faisans à l'Epicurienne
Asperges glacées
Salade Napolitaine
Salade de Saisons

———————

Gelées des Liqueurs
Bavaroise d'Orange
Crèmes à la Vanille
Chartreuse à l'Impériale
Crème à la Venetienne
Gelées des Fruits
Pâtisseries

On the raised dais at the end of the ballroom was a buffet and here, throughout the evening and early morning, waiters supplied the choicest of refreshments to the assembled guests:

Tea Coffee
Still Lemonade
Champagne Cup
Claret Cup
French bread and butter
Parisian Cakes
Petits fours
Petits Scones
Chocolate and Bonbons
Grapes Tangerines
Bananas
Ices Raspberry Vanilla
Beef Tea on departure

An evening for John and Hannah to remember as they returned to the isolated stone Workhouse in the early hours of the morning, and the sleeping pauper inmates and tramps for whose care they were responsible.

On another occasion John Warrington was entertained most lavishly with other civic dignitaries by the wealthy Councillor Herbert Partington, at his house, Talbot House, in Talbot Road, Glossop. *The Glossop Chronicle* supplies us with an account of the evening:

"The company all told, numbered nearly 30, and a more enjoyable evening they

never experienced. *The gathering was in every respect eminently successful and pleasurable. The members were received at seven and shortly afterwards sat down to dinner.*

The floral decorations of the table were very tasteful, being chiefly a charming mixture of white and crimson flowers.

The dainty red shades used over the lighting arrangements were in harmony with the general scheme of decoration.

Opening out of the Dining room was the Conservatory stocked with orchids, azaleas and other plants which was a mass of bloom, whilst from the hall came the strains of the orchestral band. The menu was as follows:

Hors d'Oeuvre Varié
Crème à la Palestine
Turbot Bouillé Sauce de Crevettes
Bouchées de Veau
Crème de Volaille
Gigot d'Agneau   Sauce Menthe
Pommes Nouvelles   Epinards au jus
Canard Sauvage Salade de Saison
Gelée aux Marasquins Crème au Café
Macédoine de Fruit en Gelée
Pâte de Fruit
Glaces
Laitance sur Croûtes
Fruit at Dessert

Vins
Solera 1883
Rudesheimer
Clinquot
Ponsardin 1895
Grand Vin
Chateau La Rose
Port 1870
Liqueurs
Café

At a late hour the gathering terminated, the host and hostess taking leave of their guests who would always recall the feelings of great pleasure, the night spent at this gracious house."

In June 1908 Herbert's father, Captain Edward Partington gave a luncheon to the Town's representatives and dignitaries, John Warrington among them. It was to celebrate his laying of the foundation stone of the new 'Partington Convalescent and Nurses' Home', in North Road, Glossop.

"It was to be an institution of the greatest public benefit and utility to be built, endowed and handed over to the townspeople of Glossop by Captain Edward Partington, to whom the well being of the community amongst whom he lives has always been of the closest personal interest."

The Convalescent home was to cost £7,293 with an endowment of £30,000. A leading

London architect's design was selected from the 96 sets submitted. Captain Edward Partington donated the money for the entire project. He stated in part of his speech after the luncheon that the Home was:

"For the advantage and convenience of that class of people who were unable to help themselves in case of direst necessity (hear, hear) as they knew that the institution was intended for the very poorest in the community and was not intended for those who could help themselves or could find sufficient money to get help. Anybody who went there for convalescent purposes, he thought would be happy and contented and would always remember the time spent in the institution".

The 'haute cuisine' luncheon was provided by the Manchester Catering Company.

"The luncheon table was beautifully decorated with red roses and maidenhair fern and other greenery and fine palms were grouped in several parts of the room. Musical selections were played during the magnificent luncheon".

This was the glowing report given by the Glossop Chronicle. It did not report however that when his workforce had asked their most generous benefactor for a pay rise of 6 pence a week, their employer refused, but said, *'No, but I'll build you a Convalescent Home'.*

The Home was opened in 1908. The illustrated brochure was produced in 1914. The Home was used for wounded Belgian soldiers in the First World War

Glossop Liberal supporters numbered over a thousand. They gave their support not only to Captain Edward, who was Chairman of the Peak Liberal Association, but to his sons, Herbert and Oswald. The latter was MP for the High Peak from 1900/1910.

As their reward, a thousand Liberal supporters from Glossopvale were invited to visit him and his family at his grand estate of Westwood Park in Worcestershire, bought by the family in 1901. The house was used mostly by his son Oswald when not at Carlton Terrace, his London address. Sir Edward still lived at Easton House in Glossop. A special train ran from the High Peak constituency to carry the loyal supporters down to the Midlands. The weather was fine and sunny and the crowds strolled through the grounds and took a look at the house.

Most of the family attended and it was remembered as a most enjoyable day for all concerned. Two marquees were erected in the grounds where the supporters were entertained for luncheon:

Sirloin of Beef - Horseradish Sauce
Galantine of Veal
Quarter of lamb and Mint Sauce
Steak and Kidney Pie
Pressed beef
Ox-tongue
Pigeon Pie
Veal and Ham Pie
Salad
Cherry tart with custard, Strawberry Cream
Straw Apricot Jelly Compote of Fruit
Various pastries
Cheese and biscuits
Wines   Claret Cup
Cider - Beer - Mineral water

In the late afternoon the happy party of Liberals returned to the High Peak, no doubt still discussing the wonderful grounds, the fare provided and the fashionable hats and dresses worn by the ladies. What a day to remember!

In 1912, Captain Edward Partington, became Sir Edward and in 1917, 1st Baron Doverdale of Westwood Park, Droitwich, Worcestershire.

June 22nd 1911 was the Coronation of George V and Queen Mary, but no one in Glossop need regret not being in London for it. Captain Edward and Mrs Sarah Partington gave a Grand Fête in the town's beautiful Howard Park. A large decorative Souvenir Brochure, tied with silk ribbon, was published at the expense of Captain Partington:

For the Coronation of His Majesty King George and Her Majesty Queen Mary Borough of Glossop Celebration.

"In no Town or City throughout the Country was there a more natural and generous outburst of loyalty than in the Borough of Glossop. Our town is highly honoured by the possession of leading Citizens, who right royally entertained Burgesses and their wives, Day school children and the Old people of the town. The donors presenting each Gentleman with cheques for 2 shillings and each Lady a cheque for One shilling and Sixpence."

10,000 people, including John and Hannah, accepted the invitation to the Grand Fête in Howard Park. They only attended briefly, during a break from the festivities at the Workhouse, but they noted that many 'Top Terrace' people made an appearance. Captain Edward and Sarah Partington arrived in their new motor car and drove under a great decorative arch signed 'Glossop's First Honorary Freeman bids you welcome'. Later Captain Edward planted a tree.

The Partingtons were photographed together with many *'important people'* - Messrs Platt and Ellison, two local cotton magnates, Mrs Sidebottom, whose family had run the Hadfield Mills for many years, and Mr Ollerenshaw, another local benefactor. Very shortly after this Captain and Mrs Partington became Sir Edward and Lady Partington.

Hannah and John's home, Beech House, was a modest compact house, built in local stone and designed exactly to their requirements. The interior of the house was furnished in exquisite taste. No gloom or clutter but bright white decor throughout, quite forward looking for the time.

Across the square cobbled courtyard at the rear of the house was a gate that opened onto a long, large, lush green lawn. Along the sheltered side of the lawn was a long wooden summer house with rooms either side that housed the garden furniture and games equipment.

On fine summer days Hannah dispensed tea to her friends, seated on cushioned basket chairs and sitting by a table covered with a white lace edged damask tea cloth. Tea would be brought out on a large tray. There would be thin slices of bread and butter, cucumber sandwiches, as well as a seed cake and home made biscuits.

Hannah and John lived there when they were off duty and there was a house-keeper. Towards their retirement they spent more and more time there, for although it was only three miles, it seemed a world away to them.

When John in his mid fifties began to be troubled with his heart, he was advised to retire and take life a little easier, so they decied to retire to Beech House. Unfortunately, their happiness was short-lived. After attending a social gathering of Church workers at the Norfolk Hotel in Glossop, John made his way to Glossop Station to catch the train home to Hadfield and his much loved Hannah. He became unwell and collapsed upon the platform. He was dead from a heart attack before a doctor arrived. It was the 27th November 1919 and he was 56 years old.

There had to be a large funeral as befitted his position in Glossop. The flags in the town were all flying at half mast. Hannah was frozen with grief and unable to do the many tasks expected of her; John had been her world, no one had understood her or loved her as he had done. Hannah was completely devastated. She wore nothing but black for the rest of her days.

She insisted that John be buried in one of the Wadsworth graves at Tintwistle Christ Church. She was to wait for nearly 36 years before she joined him in the same grave.

Polly and Jane rallied round. They sent for Mr Bamford, the undertaker in Station Road, and their local clergyman, who lived opposite, the greatly loved Rev. Archie White. He promised to take a Family Service at Beech House before the mourners made their way up to Tintwistle for the interment.

A good number of Masonic brethren, wearing sprigs of acacia, walked in front of the hearse, among them his friend, Willie Bowden. The four family coaches followed. Many of the houses in Hadfield Lane, Green Lane and along the long route to Tintwistle, had drawn their blinds as a mark of respect.

When the funeral procession reached Christ Church representatives from Glossop Parish Church were waiting with many other mourners. They were Ald. J Malkin (warden), Mr F Oldham, Mr N Burgess, Mr B Watkinson (sidesmen)

The bearers were the nephews of John and Hannah, Andrew Wadsworth, Len Ford and Dion Wadsworth, Len Wadsworth, Irvine Fisher and John Dewsnap, Albert and Walter Warrington

"At Tintwistle the obsequies held in the church and at the graveside were of a very impressive nature. The officiating clergymen were Rev W Dudley Dixon, Vicar of Glossop, Rev P W Seymour (curate) and Rev A C M White, Vicar of Hadfield.

At the close of the service 'The Dead March' was played on the organ by Brother J E Hall of Glossop. At the graveside all joined in a touching rendering of the hymn, 'Jesu, Lover of my soul', and the Masonic burial service was read by Bro T Swire.

Afterwards Hannah withdrew completely into Beech House. Neighbours and Polly and Jane watched over her but she seemed to prefer her own company. Social life stopped for Hannah. The house was never used as it was originally intended; it became a museum. Without her kindly husband's restraining hand Hannah reverted to her miserly ways and every penny had to be accounted for. Her housekeepers left, one by one, and somewhat slimmer, for Hannah begrudged having to feed and pay them.

Maria Wadsworth, the widow of Hannah's brother Timothy, retired as housekeeper to the Bromley family of Stoke Hall, East Stoke, Newark-upon-Trent at the end of 1920. She had lost her only daughter Ellen in 1918 - the Ellen who had helped on the Infirmary wards before she was old enough to train for Nursing at Brigg Hospital, Lincolnshire. Towards the end of the War, Ellen, now Matron of Brigg hospital, was responsible for a hospital full of wounded soldiers. She nursed continually throughout the terrible 'flu' epidemic that swept the world and country in 1918/19. When she succumbed to the virus her resistance was so low that she quickly died.

So sorrow linked Maria and Hannah. Maria came for a trial period to live with Hannah at Beech House as her housekeeper. She had saved very little money and had very few belongings. Hannah paid Maria four shillings a week and her keep when she arrived. When Maria reached 70 she was entitled to an old age pension of five shillings a week - so Hannah stopped paying Maria the four shillings a week when her 70th birthday arrived!

The arrangement was not a great success, and eventually Maria moved into the less palatial household of Polly and Arthur Wadsworth and their lively family, in their sweets and tobacconist shop in Bank Street, Hadfield.

Until she died Hannah continued to live most frugally. Even in the Nursing Home she would only take a tea of thin bread and butter in the late afternoon and that was her last meal for the day. She died, after outliving most of her contemporaries, at the age of ninety-six - and left a great deal of money behind her.

Ellen Wadsworth, matron, seated in centre, who died in 1918, seen here with some of her nurses at Brigg Hospital.

GLOSSOP IN THE EARLY 20TH CENTURY

John Warrington in his Masonic regalia.

Rev Archie White Vicar of Hadfield.
A most loved clergyman.

John heads for retirement.

Maria Wadsworth in old age.

Top, Broadbottom Mills, and bottom, Wood's Mills.

The noisy machinery deafened the operatives, so lip-reading became a necessity.

The weaving shed.

John Warrington in a church procession complete with umbrella. (With Father Dudley Hart and James Malkin)

Howard Park is decked out for the celebrations for the Coronation of George V, hosted by Captain Edward Partington, Freeman of Glossop.

Captain and Mrs Partington with Mrs Sidebottom at the Coronation celebrations.

Captain Edward Partington arrives for the celebrations in his new car.

Mr E Platt and Mr Ellison, both mill owners, arrive for the Coronation festivities.

More photographs taken at the Coronation celebrations.

Top:
Mrs Partington and friends.

Centre:
The Accident tent.

Bottom:
The local military with the public swimming baths in the background.

Some of the 10,000 people invited to the Coronation Celebrations of King George V and Queen Mary.

The fire at Bridge Mill 1899. The mill was a major employer.
It was a tragedy for the villages of Tintwistle and Hadfield.

The Great Fire at Bridge Mills,

HADFIELD.

LINES ON THE DISASTER, BY J. COLLIS.

IN Longdendale valley, amidst its hills so green
Once stood a cotton mill at the head of a stream.
It was built by the Sidebottoms' in " fifty-four "—
A family well-known to many a score.
One bright summer's morning, the first Monday in June,
This mill was on fire in the top room.
These lines they are true, although not in rhyme,
On the fifth day of June in eighteen ninety-nine,
A messenger was sent to Mersey Mills, just below,
Requesting their engine and firemen to go.
The captain at once set the buzzer to blow,
This was a signal of fire, you know.
For many miles round this was a shock,
As the fire brigade darted right away to the spot.
Oh! where are the hydrants? the words spread like a shot,
Bridge Mills all in flames and no water to be got.
They sent them to the river, a distance to go,
When they got there they found the stream was quite low.
They threw in their suction, ran pipes on the shed,
While the engine was waiting with water to spread.
Two Glossop brigades now arrived on the scene,
And took up position on the other side of the stream.
These engines were manuals, not driven by steam,
With a gallant set of men on that day was seen,
Worthy of credit, so here let it come,
Where they toiled all the day under a burning hot sun,
This mill was five storeys, surrounded by sheds,
And the fire to each room by now it was spread.
The smoke came from the windows with a rush and a roar,
As the roof fell with a crash upon the next floor.
Here thousands of people raised a deep, loud cry,

As the flames through the top now ascended the sky.
'Twas here Captain Matthews told his men to keep cool,
Though the fire is now master we must save the looms.
A message to Hyde by telegram now went,
And in a few minutes that brigade was sent.
With three in hand up Mottram road
With lightning speed those firemen rode.
The pace was too hot for such a journey to run,
The driver saw here his leading horse was done ;
He turned at the bottom and got well round,
When his horse again failed and fell to the ground.
They took it away, being all they could do
To finish the journey with the remaining two.
From Hyde to Tintwistle, a long journey to do,
Where they stationed their Maggie half-way down the brow,
With permission to use that water much higher,
It enabled the men to play well on the fire.
In two sections they worked, under a burning hot sun,
Returning to Hyde when their duty was done,
The fire was yet burning, much damage was done.
The mill was now gutted, all burnt to the ground,
The Glossop brigades were now homeward bound,
Leaving Mersey Mill engine first and last on the ground.
This gallant little engine, a smart little queen,
Danced and whistled and blew off the steam,
As though telling the captain she would empty the stream.
Without fault or failure she worked two days and one night,
Lifting the water, which she forced left and right,
To those who directed it on a spark or a light.
In those treacherous ruins, through the darkness of night,
And early next morning, as soon as daylight,
The people again gathered to witness the sight—
A sight heartrending and sad to behold,
Though witnessed by thousands, both young and old,
Who in years of the future this tale may unfold.
'Twas witnessed by rich as well as by poor,
It brought poverty and hunger to the working man's door ;
It was witnessed by the composer, one who feels sure
A greater fire was never witnessed in Longdendale valley before.

Four
FUNERAL TEAS
EDWARDIAN STYLE

At the turn of the century, Hadfield was a prosperous village, although its prosperity depended upon the state of the cotton industry. Like many other villages within Glossopvale, Hadfield was entirely dependent upon 'King Cotton' for its survival.

Due entirely to the rise of 'King Cotton', the original village of Hadfield now contained hundreds of purpose-built workers' dwellings, dominated by cotton mills, originally built for their position near the River Etherow, in the late 18th century, by John Thorley and John Turner, and later inherited by their sons. Three further generations of Sidebottoms generously supported local

Owners built millworkers' dwellings as near to the mill as possible

causes, especially in the nearby village of Tintwistle, and they married into another well-known mill-owning family, the Woods of Glossop.

Hadfield's population survived the large migration of cotton workers during the Cotton Famine followed by the influx of strike workers whenever there were 'call outs' at the Hadfield mills. The mill management never hesitated to bring in other workers from other parts of the Country to keep their looms alive!

Trouble returned in 1896 when the mill-owners of the Waterside complex, the Sidebottoms, went into liquidation and a couple of the mills were closed. This state continued for three miserable years. To add to the workers' distress, in 1899 a fire at Bridge mill, built by the Sidebottoms, destroyed the mill and with it any hopes of the mill working again.

Fortunately in the same year John Gartside & Co took over the Waterside Mills that had once been the largest cotton mill complex in Glossopvale. Once again there were 4,800 looms working and most of the working population of Hadfield were reprieved from hard times- this included the shopkeepers who made most of their living from the cotton operatives.

The Chappelle family lived in the shadow of a cotton mill. There were six in the family, father and mother and four children - a large family with only a pound a week to feed, clothe and shelter them.

Henry Chappelle had a safe job; he was a grave-digger. The cemetery was 800 feet above sea level on top of one of the steep and bleak slopes above the mill village of Hadfield, at the start of the Longdendale Valley. It provided no protection from the weather, completely

The grave digger at work

exposed to the winds coming down from Holme Moss and along the Longdendale valley. In winter it was bitterly cold and religious services were cut to a minimum to protect the mourners from the raw winds that gripped the cemetery. Even in summer when the sun was scorching the earth in the valley below, the breeze cooled the air in the cemetery. Here Henry Chappelle worked from 7.30 am to 5.30 pm every day except Sundays, sometimes Sunday if needed, but without extra pay - and he worked these hours throughout the year.

Occasionally when he arrived for work in the morning, he would find the body of a newborn infant wrapped in a cloth and placed in a cardboard shoe box under the boundary wall of the cemetery. After the next burial, when everyone had gone, he would place the small box on top of the coffin before filling in the grave. Some evenings a family would bring a dead infant to his back door - also wrapped in a small box. In the early morning Henry Chappelle would carry the sad little parcel up the hill to the cemetery and bury it whenever he could.

In winter he frequently returned home frozen with cold. His family would have warm rags and cloths in the hearth and they wrapped them around their father's arms, neck and face. Gradually he would feel the numbness fade away. His wife would hand him a glass of hot rhubarb wine. Soon his skin began to tingle and the icicles in his beard would melt into water.

After this nightly routine he was able to enjoy the hot meal Mary Chappelle always prepared for him. The children would have had their tea, but not a cooked one for their hot meal of the day was at mid day.

Lunchtimes for Henry up at the cemetery were always the same: Monday - cold meat and bread. Tuesday - hot steak and kidney pie in a basin and wrapped in a large red cloth that was taken up to the cemetery by one of his children. Wednesday - cold sausage and bread.

Thursday was a difficult day; bread and cheese. If the Superintendent's wife was in an amiable mood she might oblige by putting the piece of cheese and butter to melt in her oven and he would eat this with bread for his dinner. Other times he would eat it cold.

Friday it was bread and cheese again but it was also pay day. Henry would walk down into the village to pay for the groceries at the Hadfield Co-operative Store, and he collected the Sunday joint from the butcher's. The change he was left with had to pay the rent, buy the fuel and feed them all until the following Friday.

Before her marriage Mary Chappelle had spent several years 'in service' in Yorkshire until her Mother, on a visit to her daughter one Sunday, found her engaged in pre-soaking Monday's washing down in the cellar: Her Mother was a strict non-conformist and putting washing in to soak on a Sunday was against her religious principles. She departed back to the village and soon found her daughter a job in the Mill, away from those Pagans in Yorkshire.

Mary Chapelle helped all she could towards the family income, and her domestic training came to the rescue. Mary made it known within the village community that she would prepare 'Funeral Teas' for the folk who had neither the time nor the inclination to do this essential task. Irrespective of class the Edwardians believed in burying their dead with as much style as the 'Burial Fund' and the family purse would allow. 'Mourning Black' was essential. Drapers' shops would advertise *"Mourning Black made in two days"*. Large black veils, edged with black satin were sometimes worn by the principle women mourners. Some women mourners wore black jet or bog oak brooches with 'In Memoriam' carved upon them. The chief men mourners wore black suits and ties and black 'pot' hats. Black arm bands were worn by friends and other relatives.

Mourning memorial cards were essential to send to distant friends and relations. The bill for the cards came with the undertaker's account. They came in various styles. The most expensive were small black and gold-edged cards that cost 2/ 6d per dozen.

There were pretty mauve silk bookmarks with a suitable verse printed upon them to place in a family bible. The cards contained the name of the deceased, the date of their demise and a suitable religious verse:

'We loved her, ah no tongue can tell
How much we loved her, and how well
But God in mercy thought it best
To take her to Himself to rest
Peace, Perfect Peace'.

or

The winter of trouble is past
The storms of affliction are o'er;
His struggle is ended at last,
And sorrow & death are no more.

A death in the family, hard though it may be, did not necessitate losing more than one day's pay at work and this applied to women as well as men. But no woman worth her salt would fail to have a substantial funeral tea for the mourners. *'Burying them with 'am'* was a necessary ritual for the family pride. The hierarchy of village women looked down upon *'bought cakes'* or *'bought bread'* for guests.

Mary Chappelle's clients provided the money for the ingredients. She charged a shilling for preparing the Tea in her home and delivering it to the house of mourning. Mary's funeral menu list:

One dozen loaves (12 lbs flour)
Tea cakes (6 lbs flour)
One seed cake
One currant cake
One boiled ham

The spread would be carefully packed into a wicker clothes basket and Mary, helped by her daughters, would carry it to the back door of the house of mourning where they would unpack the food and be paid the fee. Then, before taking their leave, mother and daughters would view the body to avoid offence to the bereaved family. Viewing the dead was the 'done' thing in Edwardian times. It was not thought undesirable at all, but as a mark of respect to the deceased for people to call at the house of mourning and ask to see 'them'.

A knock on the front door would be answered, the caller greeted with *"Come in, love"* and shown into the front room where the body lay. The curtains were drawn - just as neighbours would draw their front curtains on the day of the funeral as a mark of respect. Sometimes there were people already in the candle-lit room. Together they would admire the beauty of the coffin and its brass handles and the skill of the needlework upon the fine cotton shroud worn by the deceased.

Probably the deceased, in her prime and with her eyesight good, had worked for hours on the elaborately embroidered, crochet-trimmed shroud. When finished it was carefully wrapped in black tissue paper and lovingly placed in the bottom of the family chest until needed. As she got older she would constantly remind her family where the shroud was kept, in case they forgot and the many hours of needlework should be 'wasted' and not go on show.

Viewing the dead was conducted in whispers, then they would quietly leave. Fortunately the Chappelle daughters, Liddy and Nancy found this 'viewing the dead' quite fascinating. The only time the girls were apprehensive was when the body to view had been involved in an argument with a railway engine when taking a short cut across the railway track on his way home. The girls were greatly relieved to find that 'he' had only a few scratches to his face and a small hole in his chin - the rest of the body was well covered.

Young Irish Catholic bodies were dressed in scarlet robes. In their right hand was placed a small wooden hammer to knock upon the Gates of Heaven; in their left hand a shiny new penny to pay for their admission.

The cooking of the 'Funeral Tea' took Mary Chappelle all day. By the time the children arrived home from school, the cottage living room was like a furnace from the heat emitted by the coal-fired iron kitchen range. Mary was rosy-cheeked and her hair hung in wisps caused by her labour. The children munched on warm oven-bottom cakes filled with melting butter and cheese for tea. Another treat for the family was the local version of 'Chorley cake'. If there was any spare pastry at the end of the baking session Mary rolled it into a circle and placed a small handful of currants and sugar into the centre. She drew the circle of dampened pastry together, turned it over and rolled it again into a circle. It was cooked in the oven until golden brown. When it was warm it was smeared with butter and cut into pieces for immediate consumption.

Mary's reputation was made on her 'Funeral Teas'. She was further able to supplement the family income by 'weekend baking' for regular clients. Several mill workers relied upon Mary Chappelle to supply them with their weekend 'bread balm cakes' and a 'sweet cake' for Sunday tea. The children delivered these, fresh from the oven, on Saturday afternoons, to various local households where the woman would not stoop to buying 'shop bought' bread and cake for weekends. There was a strict code of *'dos and don'ts'* amongst the village working women. One of these was that it was *'not done'* to buy from the confectioners for the weekend. During the week it was tolerated to indulge in using them but not for Sunday tea. Women who served *'shop bought cake'* were noted and disapproved of, despite the fact that the standards of the local bakers were very high.

Sunday was the one day of the week when the Chappelle family all gathered together for dinner and tea. Whenever possible there was a modest roast joint with Yorkshire puddings and vegetables, followed by a fruit pie. When the roast was smaller than usual the family were served with generous portions of Yorkshire pudding and gravy first. The saying was *"Them 'as 'ad most puddin' shall 'ave most meat"* in the hope was that they would feel so full that they would not need as much meat with their vegetables.

Thick oxtail soup was an economical weekday dish that the family enjoyed. The butcher chopped the tail for her. When Mary got home she would wash the tail and put the pieces into a large stewpot. She added chopped onion and chopped carrot and pearl barley. It was seasoned, water added and the lid put on. It was cooked slowly all day in the fire oven - and when the flesh broke away easily it was ready to eat.

A sheep's head provided another good meal, despite the usual joke when the head was bought - the butcher would ask his customer if she wanted the eyes to be left in the head *'to see them through the week.'* The head was thoroughly cleaned and placed in a large stewpot.

Chopped onions, leeks, swede and carrots were added, with a good handful of barley for thickening. The head was cooked slowly until the scraps of meat left on the head were cooked. The head was removed and the scraps of meat were scraped off and returned to the pot. The head was saved for anyone who liked to suck the goodness from it. The pot was returned to the fire bar and the final act was to drop suet dumplings into the simmering stew.

Other weekdays she would make a thick pea soup from dried split peas. Another favourite, when the weather was very cold, Mary would buy cheap tough 'shin' beef and cook it in the oven all day with butter beans that absorbed the juice from the meat.

A greengrocer's cart called at the Chappelle home late on Saturday night. Being a kind-hearted man he would find 'Saturday night bargains' for Mary. It might be an apron full of apples at 2d a pound or a generous amount of oranges for a few pence. When rhubarb was plentiful he would bring her a large bundle for he knew she made the warming rhubarb wine for her husband

When the eldest child, Maria reached twelve she was able to work half-time in the mill for 3/3d a week. The children took an examination at school which, if they were successful, allowed them to work part-time in the mill. Maria the eldest Chappelle daughter had been working a couple of years in the mill by the time Nancy and Liddy began working half-time.

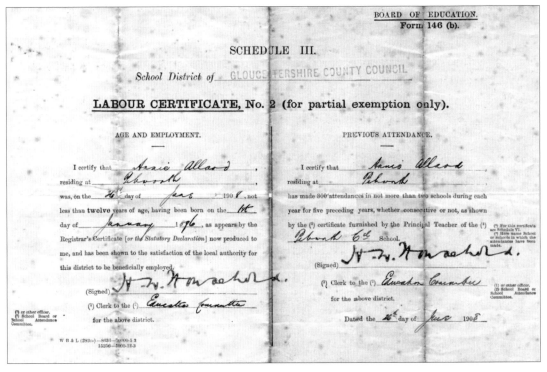

A Labour certificate for a young girl aged twelve allowing her to work.

This was their daily routine: 5.30 am: Rise to get to the mill for the 6 am start, for if they were late they were fined. On the way to the mill they would drop in their tea cans, containing tea and sugar, to a Mrs Shepley who undertook to supply the milk and bring the newly brewed tea to the mill for the 8am breakfast half hour. For supplying milk and delivering the cans to the mill every day for six days, she charged 4d. Her milkman had to be reliable. He had to be bright and early for Mrs Shepley or he would encounter her wrath and be called scathingly *'nothin' but a milk puddin' milkman'!* Many years later it was found that tea leaves contained some herbal qualities that gave the workers a small protection from infection as well as being a mild stimulant.

All the operatives had their own tin box in which they kept their food to protect it from the hot, moist atmosphere in the mill. The tea was delivered at 8am. The girls opened their tins to discover a 'balm cake' each with a piece of bacon tucked in between. This was munched and enjoyed as they sat on a large wicker skip and they used their tea can lid as a cup for the hot tea. The folk who were not so fortunate in their housekeepers had to manage with just bread and margarine or bread and jam for breakfast. In some households, bread and jam had an unhappy knack of turning up at dinner-times as well .

After breakfast, work was resumed until 12.30pm when Maria would signal to Nancy and Liddy to run home and fetch their dinners. They were packed in an oblong wicker basket made with a handle running across the centre. There was a wicker lid and when this later became too worn to use, embroidered, lace-trimmed cloths would cover the food for its journey to the mill. Mrs Chappelle would have ready three basins which contained hot steak and kidney puddings, or a tasty meat and potato pie, known locally as 'tater pie'. If she baked one large meat and potato pie this was wrapped in a large red cloth and carried by one girl, the other carrying the plates and spoons in the basket.

If funds allowed there might also be an apple pie in the basket or a blackberry and apple turnover. Nancy and Liddy always had their dinner with their sister before they rushed up to the village school for 1.30 until 4.30pm.

At first Liddy and Nancy enjoyed sitting, legs dangling, upon a skip with their plates balancing upon their knees and eating their meal together. Their enthusiasm soon dimmed as they found the work hard and the conditions they worked under so harsh. The pungent smell of oil that coated the wooden floors made them feel nauseated The floors could be very slippery. The deafening noise of the machinery continued relentlessly throughout the shift - Liddy and Nancy were forced to acquire the skill of lip reading.

The temperature in the spinning and weaving sheds was kept at a moist 65 to 70 degrees or the cotton threads would break. Buckets of icy river water were sometimes thrown upon the floor to create the moist air. The fact that operatives worked in a real fire hazard never occurred to them. The needs of 'King Cotton' took priority over everything.

The inside of some of the 'sheds' resembled a snow scene with the cotton waste dancing around and clinging to the operatives. There was a great deal of dust from the oily cotton fibres. At the end of the shift, when the workforce spilled out into the Mill yard, it looked as if most the workers had been caught up in a snowstorm.

The women in their serviceable thick grey shawls about their heads and shoulders made for the food shops. The men poured into the nearest public house, never far from a mill.

The women had a choice of at least seven bread and confectionary shops that served succulent meat and potato pies, or small gravy filled meat pies. There were three chip shops spaced evenly along the road. There were many butchers' shops, a tripe shop and a pork butcher's that sold slices of hot roast pork in gravy. The only drawback was the small amount of money available in their purses - buying ready cooked food could soon run away with the week's food money. On Friday pay night the money flowed into the Station Road shops.

It was hard enough to manage their money from Friday to Friday, but at one time the workforce were paid every fortnight and there were several 'turn outs' by the operatives until the wages were paid weekly.

When Liddy and Nancy went to school in the morning, which they did on alternate weeks, they would rush out of school at 12 noon to collect their dinners from home and take them to the mill so that they would be ready to start work at 1.30 until 6 pm.

Friday was pay day. A Mrs Bramhall who lived near the mill undertook to make meat and potato pies in large saucers, and buns to order, for dinner time. The price of one of these succulent pies was two pence. On Fridays, the two younger sisters would run all the way to Mrs Bramhall's house to collect the first of the dozen or so pies that she had ready for despatch to the mill.

There were no afternoon breaks for tea, despite the oppressive moist heat in the mill. To quench their thirst the girls usually saved some cold tea from the breakfast half hour and would drink this while they worked. If one of the operatives became unwell, the other girls would hold her tea-can over a hot steam pipe and try to warm up the stale tea to make them a warm drink.

Pay for part-time work at the mill was 3/3d a week. Holidays, without pay, were Easter Monday, Whit Saturday and Christmas Day. The mills closed down during 'Wakes Week' for repairs and to overhaul the machinery. For 51 weeks of the year the mill machinery clattered away both day and night. For one week of the year the looms were silent.

But there was no pay for 'Wakes Week'. It had to be prepared for. All year round one worker at the mill took sixpence a week from the workers so that on 'broken pay' week, which was 'Wakes Week', there would be enough money to pay out to the workers for their financial survival during the week without pay. The collector took the interest that the bank gave on the total sum of money saved throughout the year, his reward for doing the weekly collection.

When the Chappelle daughters all worked full-time they were allowed a shilling a week for spending money and it was half of this that they gave to the 'broken pay' week fund.

The extra money Mary Chappelle earned took the knife edge off their poverty when her family were all young and unable to work. As her girls grew into young women she acquired a sewing machine and embarked upon family dressmaking. She would stay up all night if necessary with her sewing until the girls were competent enough to assist their mother, for most of the garments were for them.

They each had shoes at 2/11d a pair from Swire's shoe shop in Station Road. They learnt to trim their own hats and there was much laughter as they exchanged opinions upon the finished products and finally obtained their mother's approval. They were each bought a pair of stockings and a pair of white cotton gloves to complete their finery.

'Best clothes', especially shoes, were a passport to Church and Sunday school, and invitations to the many social events within the small community, like the Co-op Galas and Summer Day trips, and parading with their church at 'The Sermons'. 'Village Concerts' and 'Church Socials' kept them well entertained during the long northern winters.

The first thing the girls did when they returned home from a social event was to run up the stairs and take off their finery. There was no sitting around in 'best' clothes as in some of the houses in the village. Mary insisted that *'best clothes'* would lose their shape and skirts would *'bag'* if *'sat about in'* too much. They always had to obtain permission from their mother to wear their 'best clothes'.

Mary Chappelle bought all her bargain remnants for sewing from 'Ted's Stall'. This was a wooden hut that stood at the top of the road by the Waterside Mill complex. He sold remnants of cloth, patchwork pieces for quilts and flannelette for nightdresses. Ted was open for a short time on Fridays and Saturdays. There was such a frantic scramble from the women buying the remnants that Mary used to accumulate small change, because those folk with the correct money always were served first. At Christmas he would sell large dolls for sixpence. Childrens' frocks were also on sale for sixpence.

In late Spring the three girls would walk to declare their faith under their own religious banner at the 'Sermons' when everyone within a church or chapel community walked in procession around the village. (except the Catholics) It was an excellent opportunity for showing off their new finery.

Tintwistle Brass Band, affectionately known as 'Tinsel Crash', led the village parade. The many onlookers who lined the route enjoyed the music and the yearly fashion parade.

On the 'Treat' days, waggonettes of excited pleasure-seeking young folk would depart in the early morning for pastures new. It mattered not if everybody had to unload for the numerous hills whilst the men and boys pushed the waggonette. They had such fun and laughter loading up again and seeing that no one was left behind. Gone were the cares of the year and the dark bitter mornings; the fetching and carrying for mother and all those corpses. For this day life was carefree and golden.

The following year the girls and their mother took part in a summer train excursion from Hadfield to the fashionable seaside resort of Southport in Lancashire with the Sunday school.

The excited party left Hadfield Station at 6.30 am and arrived in Southport at 9 o'clock. For seven hours Southport was theirs. Lord Street looked wonderful with its long rows of shady trees and well furnished shop windows, full of very expensive items. It was whispered among the group of visiting ladies, as they strolled along gazing into the windows of the fashionable clothes shops, that this was the resort where wealthy Manchester businessmen kept their mistresses!

The seashore was a great attraction, the water chute and the flying machine, the lake and the booths, the motor cars and the pier. By 4.30 they were glad to take a short rest; it was time to do full justice to the ample fare provided at the Temperance Institute. Weary, but happy, they reached Hadfield at 10.15 pm after a day to be remembered.

Another year, the same party of helpers and the Sunday school travelled by train in a 'saloon carriage' to Southport, where they had both dinner and tea at Fisher's Café in Lord Street. They visited and explored the Botanical Gardens before returning home at 10pm. In future years there were other destinations for the Chappelle ladies - Chester and Cleethorpes.

Faced in later years with the Cotton slump, the family kept up their tradition of hard work. The three sisters went into service in Manchester to keep their parents free from the fear of having to end up in the Workhouse, a nightmare for so many old people in the early part of the 20th century.

Hadfield, Hollingworth and Tintwistle.
OS Map 1898

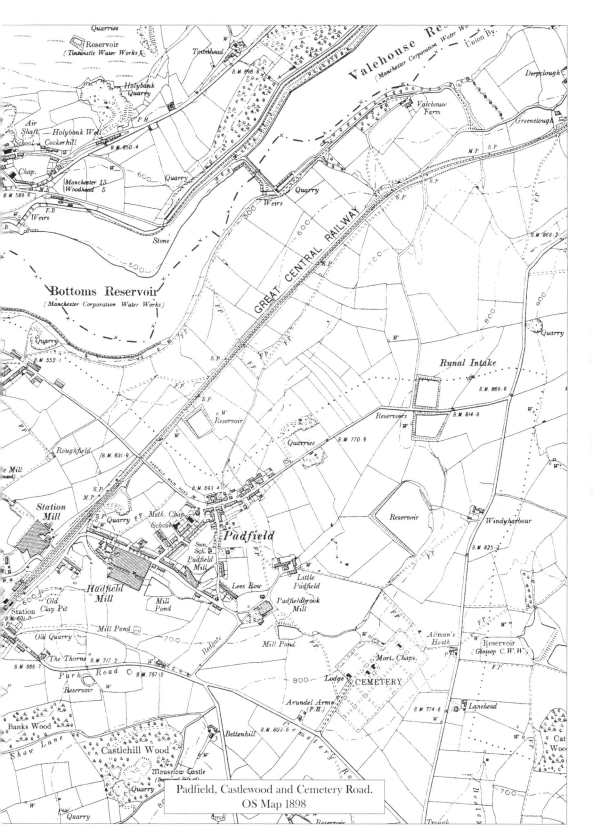

Padfield, Castlewood and Cemetery Road.
OS Map 1898

Coronation celebrations in the Spinning Room at the mill 1911.

Tintwistle Band.

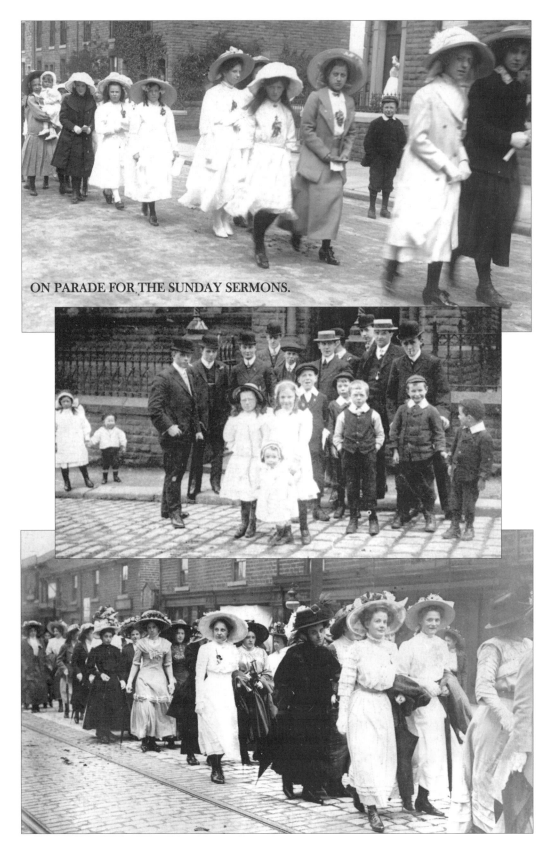

ON PARADE FOR THE SUNDAY SERMONS.

Five

MAGGIE MORSE'S CHILDHOOD
MEMORIES OF HADFIELD

God help the poor, who in lone valleys dwell,
Or by the hills where whin and heather grow
Theirs is a story sad indeed to tell;
Yet little cares the world, and less to know,
About the toil and want they undergo.
The wearing loom must have them up at morn;
They wake till worn out nature will have sleep;
They taste, but are not fed. The snow drifts deep
Around the fireless cot and blocks the door;
The night storm howls a dirge across the moor.....

Samuel Bamford.

Hadfield had one long main road, imaginatively called Station Road, leading down from the railway station to the crossroads, and then on to the Waterside Mill complex.

There were three main public houses from the top of the street to the bottom, The Palatine, The Mason's Arms and the Commercial Inn, along with several beer sellers.

The long road was filled with shops; people rarely needed to go to Glossop on the tram or train for anything except the Glossop market which took place on Fridays. There was John Wilde, the blacksmith, at Nos 73 and 75, Joseph Billinge, the saddler, at No 108 Station Road. There were five butchers and one pork butcher, plus a tripe shop at 142. Nine bakers were available, Ellis Wright at 27, William Cannon at No 7, Miss A Fielding at 52, Harry Garner at No 17, with William Greaves at 103 Station Road, Samuel Woodhouse Chadwick at 99, the Misses Mary and Sarah Ellen Haigh at 90, William Hoylands at 116 and William Rutherford at 52.

There were several grocers, Thomas Braddock at 111 and William Cannon at No 7, with H. Etchells at 91. There were at least two greengrocers. There was a sub branch of the Manchester & County Bank Ltd, and a post office and stationers run by Mrs Wright at no 72

You could consult a solicitor, Edward Percy Ireland at number 91. There were two doctors, if should you need them. Mrs Mary Cocks was a nurse found at 36, Station Road.

There was a busy ironmonger's shop, smelling of paraffin and firelighters. A most necessary shop was the pawnbroker's shop and there was Miss Bentham's gem of a toyshop at 47, which was a darkened cavern of delight, smelling of celluloid and painted tin. There were two sweet and tobacco shops, and a watchmaker at No. 31.

A large branch of the Co-operative Society, with a butcher's, grocer's and draper's department, reigned supreme in the middle of Station Road. 'Divi' was an important part of the housekeeper's existence and every member of the family knew their number by heart. There was also a clothing or household money scheme that many families depended upon. The women paid sixpence or a shilling each week and they were allowed 20 times that amount to spend immediately. It took 20 weeks to pay it back before you could take out another credit.

Fish and chip shops were found at 34, 21 & 69. There were many shoe shops that repaired and sold shoes and John Swire had a clog shop at 114 which sold and repaired clogs. If a lady fancied a new hat there was James Livesley & Co, milliner, at 104. A clothier and outfitter was at 121, a tailor at No. 29. Miss Agnes Howarth was a dressmaker at 64. Hairdressers were to be found at No 40 and 106 Station Rd .

When a photograph was needed Ernest Batty was at 109. If you needed new teeth there was an 'Artificial Masticators' maker at 65 Station road. For those who could afford a master painter and decorator, Frederick Bismark Fisher traded at No 25. A watchmaker, Thomas Hall, resided at 31, and an umbrella maker, John William Webb, at No. 70.

If work and money were plentiful you could buy a piano from John James Roberts at 89 Station Rd. There was John Richardson's chemist's, and a herbalist shop belonging to Peter Johnson at 37. When you needed to be buried, Frederick Howarth undertaker and furniture dealer was at number 6.

Tucked away off the top of Station Road was the recently built St Andrews Church of England. The Church School was a little further down the road, nearer to the station. At the other end of the village was an established Catholic church, St. Charles, and a Convent school built by Lord Howard.

The large Independent Chapel rose from the top of one of the steep sided streets off Station Road aptly named Bank Street. The chapel led to the original part of the village with its small stone built Old Hall and ancient Village Cross.

Down from the Village Cross was Hadfield Road where anyone who was anyone in Hadfield lived, alongside the parson and the two doctors.

Aloof from all this, by a mile or so, was a large gracious house with extensive gardens called Mersey Bank. The house was built in 1862 by Mr W. Rhodes, a wealthy millowner, who originated from Tintwistle. On the death of Mr Rhodes senior in 1883, Edward Platt, another mill owner bought Mersey Bank and lived there until he died in 1915. Edward Platt built Hadfield Library and Public Hall in memory of his father.

Mr Rhodes owned the Mersey Mill and later Hadfield Mill which employed 1,000 workers in 1897. On his death his son George Wood Rhodes took over the Mersey Mill Company and his two other sons, William and Herbert, ran the Padfield Mill. The latter were both Mayors of Glossop. Herbert Rhodes donated £2,000 towards the building of the Victoria Hall in Glossop, as did Captain Edward Partington another well known local benefactor.

Maggie Morse was born at the beginning of the new century, when Queen Victoria was still on the throne. She was born at Rose Grove, Charlesworth but spent her childhood and youth in the Derbyshire mill village of Hadfield and neighbouring Padfield. The family moved to Hadfield when Walter Morse found work to help build an elaborate clock tower at the prosperous Etherow Bleach Works in nearby Woolley Bridge.

Maggie was the third to be born into a happy family, ably supported by father, Walter. Their mother Isobella stayed at home, rearing the three children Jim, Elsie and Maggie, and another baby on the way. But tragedy struck the young family when their father, Walter, collapsed on his way home from work one winter evening. He was dead by the time his workmates got him home. He was in his early forties. Maggie's mother, Isobella, was seven months pregnant, left entirely responsible for three small children and one soon to arrive. Life became very grim after that terrible day.

Somehow Isobella managed to keep the family together until her baby was born. Maggie's mother used to tell her in later years how folk then pulled together in adversity. When a woman was confined, the neighbours would rally round. Everything had to be spanking clean. One neighbour would clean the bedroom. The mother-to-be was given 'a good wash down' and her hair brushed before the doctor or midwife arrived. A clean loop of towel was tied to the back of the bed for her to pull on when the painful contractions arrived. The labour and delivery would be left to the midwife.

Another neighbour would take the family washing, they would wash, iron and return the clothes back 'aired' and ready to wear. Someone else would do the shopping. Somebody would do the cooking. Another neighbour would tend to the other children such as bathing them and putting them to bed.

After the birth, all the mother had to do was to get well and rest for a few days. The neighbours were only thankful that all had gone well. There was no such thing as being paid; nobody wanted it. They all helped each other whenever they could.

Then there were superstitions about a new born baby. When a woman was delivered of a baby, the first thing anyone did was to place a silver coin in the baby's right hand and to clasp its fingers around it. If the baby held on to it, it was supposed to be well off for the rest of its life. If the baby released the coin it was considered unlucky.

Until the mother had been 'churched' after the birth, she was not encouraged to take the baby over the threshold of anyone's home - nothing but misfortune would follow her and the household she visited. The churching service, held in Church by the parson, sounded as if the mothers had deliberately been to hell and back and were granted a reprieve from their unclean ways. Most mothers didn't listen, they just wanted to be accepted again in other folks' homes.

If a baby died or was still born the baby was wrapped and put in a box and put over the cemetery wall where one of the gravediggers would find it and bury it when he had the chance.

Doctors were a luxury but sometimes necessary, especially at a difficult birth or a grave illness. At the other end of the spectrum, of course, they also would remove an adult's aching tooth, when they were desperate with pain and came to see him in the surgery. Most women put a tiny amount of money away each week in case they had to call the doctor who would always come in those days, day or night.

Every bottle of medicine was put down, every visit noted, and when the patient recovered the doctor would send a bill. He employed a collector who came round every week to collect the money. Some people would give him 3d to 6d a week. Doctors could not afford to turn patients away or refuse even a small payment. The surgery hours were 6 days a week, Monday to Saturday:

Morning	9 am - 10 am
Afternoon	3 pm - 4.30 pm
Evening	6 pm - 8 pm

In the home there were more primitive ways of removing teeth, especially for young children's milk teeth. A senior member of the family would tie fine strong, thread around the victim's tooth, who was instructed where to stand, somewhere near the fireplace. The fine thread was securely wound around the knob of the open heavy oven iron door. With a sharp slam of the door many such troublesome teeth were removed. After a loud yell of pain and resentment, order was restored within the family.

Women 'put up' with their complaints. Modesty prevented anything 'down below', like prolapses, from being repaired. Anaemia was treated with smelling salts and pills and potions bought from the chemist or herbalist. Edwardian society was a patriachial society. Women were an underprivileged group. In 1901 a married woman could be expected to bear nine or ten children, yet talking about sex with anyone was taboo. A woman submitted and endured this part of her marriage - many mothers would say to their daughters that she must never refuse her husband, for he might stray to another woman and the blame would be the wife's.

Menstrual periods were dark womenly secrets. Some mothers failed to warn their daughters of the start of menstrual periods. She waited until her young daughter woke up, quite terrified, in a blood stained bed. Along with the hushed whispers which surrounded pregnancy, ignorance and prejudice walked hand in hand, like the myth that it was dangerous for women to wash their hair during menstruation.

Sanitary towels were usually old towelling strips safety-pinned into the gusset of their drawers. It was a constant dread that the menstrual flow would stain their day clothes, even the thought of it would bring a humiliated blush to the feminine cheek. After use the towels were soaked in cold water and salt before being boiled in an old pan and secretly stored away in a drawstring cotton bag until needed.

Many women suffered from debility, generally caused by undernutrition and anaemia. Their idea of 'building themselves up' was a little extra bread and butter and 'milk pobs'. When faced with a shortage of food in the home the father was served first, then the children, with mother eating whatever was left.

If sheer necessity forced her out to earn money, they were usually hard, underpaid jobs. Their biological make-up made women unreliable according to many employers. A good education for girls was considered wasted by many working families as she would only marry and have a family.

The care of children in the home was the woman's responsibility. She was also the household manager and responsible for feeding her family. Maternity and child welfare services were in their infancy, and only then as a result of middle class and upperclass women doing 'good works' in the slums of cities. In the East End of London, some of the well-to-do ladies paid for a respectable woman to visit women with families living in one room. She was known to these women as 'The Puddin' Lady' for she helped them to prepare a nourishing meal with the bare amount of utensils that she found in their sparse accommodation.

When the Country went to war with the Boers, the Inspector of Recruiting for the Army had the greatest difficulty in obtaining sufficient numbers of men of satifactory physique for service in the South African War. Nationally 40% of recruits were rejected. The state of Britain's fighting fodder was considered to be well below standard, with bad teeth, stunted growth and heart defects, as well as poor sight and hearing. In 1902 the minimum height of the infantry soldiers was reduced to 5 ft. It was concluded by the War Office that these

THE NATIONAL
TRAINING SCHOOL FOR COOKERY,
South Kensington, S.W.

RECIPES

FOR

PLAIN COOKERY,

AS TAUGHT IN THE LECTURE ROOM

OF THE SCHOOL,

'N THE INTERNATIONAL INVENTIONS EXHIBITION, 1885.

PREPARED BY
MRS. CHARLES CLARKE,
THE LADY SUPERINTENDENT.

LONDON:
WILLIAM CLOWES AND SONS, LIMITED,
'NTERNATIONAL INVENTIONS EXHIBITION, SOUTH KENSINGTON,
AND 13, CHARING CROSS, S.W.
1885.

Station Road, Hadfield.

unfortunate men had been reared on such a poor diet due to poor housekeeping and a lack of cooking skills. Women were ignorant of what foods were needed. It never seemed to occur to these higher authorities that poor families could not afford a good diet!

The powers-that-be decided that something must be done; a committee was formed to look into the matter, and produced a *"Report of the Inter-Departmental Committee on Physical Deterioration"*. One of the many outcomes of this report was to insist that domestic science be introduced into the school curriculum for girls. The result, they hoped, would be that the next generation of young women would improve their standards of homemaking.

The object was to ensure for the working man a wholesome meal 'nicely prepared' which will supply the nourishment he needs to do a hard day's work. The lassitude produced by bad food and hard work is the constant source of the craving for stimulants which drives the working man to a public house.

(The National Training School for Cookery)

The Board of Education now made serious attempts during a girl's education to provide lessons in cookery, sewing and child care. At first they were for a limited period of six weeks only. Eventually domestic science became part of most girls' school syllabus. Unfortunately it was not extended to the brighter girls who were encouraged to take 'serious' subjects.

When Maggie's mother, Isabella, was safely delivered of a son, Harold, she was forced to use a child minder and go out to work. Mill work was not possible because of the hours, so it was scrubbing and cleaning, and washing for other people.

She would walk up Marlow Brow, the steep hill out of Hadfield, and 'over the top' to the road that led down North Road into Glossop for 8am. When she reached the house, Beechwood, in North road, she was let into a basement outside washing cellar by a servant. Here she washed the household clothes. She boiled the bed linen and cotton underwear, put the clothes through the heavy wooden rollers of the mangle into a tub full of blue rinsing water, and 'dollyed' the clothes to release the soap suds.

With a long wooden stick Isobella hauled out the washing into a second tub of rinsing water. Once more the clothes were put through the mangle before the clothes were piled into a large wicker clothes basket and pegged outside to dry, or hung out across the washing lines in the other cellars. Some of the linen was dipped through 'hot water starch' made by one of the maids beforehand. If the washing was dry, she was expected to fold it ready for ironing.

Isobella would be kept busy until 2 pm with nothing but water from the cellar tap that she cupped her hands under to get a drink. Wearily she would climb the steep back steps and be paid two shillings before she walked back the three miles to the top of North Road and down the steep hill back into Hadfield.

Isobella scrubbed and cleaned in other wealthy houses on other weekday mornings. Working from 9am until well after mid-day, she was paid one shilling and sixpence. But still she couldn't manage. In Maggie's words:

"After a little while mother found it impossible to manage and she had to ask for what went under the name of 'parish relief'. Outdoor Relief was allowed to widows with legitimate children dependent upon them for the first six months after their bereavement. God pity you

when it came to that. My mother carried the baby, and I clung to her skirts, as we walked over to Glossop Workhouse. We faced the Board of Guardians. A more heartless and inhuman lot will never be known again."

It was in an imposing, awe-inspiring room, full of expensive oak furniture and rich furnishings. A huge log fire gave off golden rays; firescreens protected the prosperous guardians from scorching their well-upholstered rears. The large highly polished table had heavy round pewter ink pots dotted along it.

In this majestic room the very poor applied for 'Outdoor Relief' when every other means of providing food and warmth was exhausted. From a separate entrance the poor and needy came through a tall narrow oak door and took their place behind the marble topped counter that was locked either side by a sturdy pew-like door. Here they stood and faced the Poor Law Guardians. They were a formidable collection of prosperous, well fed worthies, who guarded the ratepayers' money against the financial inadequacies of the poor.

The Chairman sat on a throne-like chair in the centre on a raised dias. On either side of him sat other important officers. Near the 'top table' sat various members of the Board of Guardians. In one corner of the imposing setting was a small box-like section for the Press.

"Mother struggled to state her case because she felt so intimidated - and she promised to dwell on the advice and instructions given to her by the Members of the Board of Guardians."

She was told she would have to report back every week and state everything that she had purchased during that week, before she could receive further financial help.

"The Relieving Officer sat at a small table near the Pauper end of the Board Room. He had a canvas bag with the money in it and an open ledger upon the table. He looked sternly at Mother, as if it was his own money that he was parting with. He said "very well" and tossed the few shillings over to her.

If mother bought what she thought was a necessity, such as a half pound of tough shin meat, the Guardians called shin beef a luxury, and the next week when Mother and I went we were told that we could manage on less money and promptly knocked 1/- off that week. Woe betide you if you asked them not to reduce it. They would think nothing of threatening to take the lot off you."

When Maggie started school there was a scheme started to help the very poor. It was a free breakfast of coffee and bread:

"Whenever I smell coffee it takes me back to those far off days; I don't know who started the scheme but they earned the eternal blessing of quite a few mothers".

Many times the family went to bed hungry and cold as there was no coal for the fire, so there was no hot food, even in the depth of a bitter northern winter. *"Funnily a full stomach makes you feel warm as well",* Maggie recalled. Her mother went hungry more than the children. The neighbours sometimes gave the Morse family 'left overs' but there was never enough to go round, so the children were fed first.

"It was a matter of luck, you ate or you didn't, it depended on how lucky you were. It was no use asking for help because some poor devils seemed worse off than we were, especially if they had a bad 'manager'. Funnily enough, people tried to share what they could

Board of Guardians Room, Bridgewater Hospital, Patricroft, Lancashire.
Above: The room where the Board of Guardians sat to consider outdoor relief.
Below: Where the poor stood to ask for it.

when they could. There was a form of snobbery about the very poor like us. Working class people did look down on us. Mother did not like this for she felt that it wasn't our fault."

Despite grinding poverty, Maggie's mother believed that 'cleanliness was next to Godliness.' When Isobella washed the children's hair, she used to turn on the cold water tap over the 'slopstone' in the kitchen and duck their heads under the cold tap and wash their hair with household soap.

The children's clothes were washed in a similar manner. All the children went to bed very early on Sunday nights so that their clothes would be dried and ready to wear in the morning, if they were lucky. In the winter the underclothes were sometimes a touch damp when they went off to school on Monday morning. *"The amount of clothes we had all depended on what mother could afford to buy for us at Jumble Sales."*

Their bedsteads were iron with wooden slats across from head to foot. Upon these slats was placed a straw palliasse. They were *"ruddy prickly"*, according to Maggie, for the prickles came through the rough twill sheets that covered them.

"When the straw beds were scrapped we had 'flock' mattresses. Eventually the wooden slats gave way to wire mattresses. They were fine for jumping up and down upon. It was just like a trampoline.

Downstairs the floors were stone flags and were scrubbed 3 times a week to keep them 'anything like'. The floors were scrubbed and donkey stone was rubbed onto the damp flags; it was 'smoothed over' with a well wrung out floor cloth. There were three colours of donkey stone to choose from, mustard yellow, white and cream. The donkey stones were usually given away by the Rag and Bone man in exchange for old rags and other bits and pieces. He used to do the rounds of the village once a week.

Everybody had their own way of stoning the floors. Some of them would yellow stone so far round and colour the centre white. The yellow band was smoothed over with a damp cloth for the final touch and the centre was done in squiggles and swirls to make it fancy."

Thursday was cleaning night when the 'fire irons' were polished. They consisted of a fender, a pair of tongs and a shovel and poker. For a long time fire irons were made of brass. After a while brass went out of fashion and a flat tapped steel set took over. This was a cheap form of steel minus chromium. It had a dull, flat appearance that needed a great deal of elbow grease to obtain a shine. The Morse children had to burnish the fire irons until they shone like silver. On Thursday evenings they were polished and were put away to re-emerge in their glory on Saturday after dinner. On Saturday night with a nice clean house, the 'fire irons' looked splendid with the fire-light shining on them.

There was a solitary paraffin lamp on the scrubbed deal table downstairs; the rest of the house depended upon candle power. Gas was out of the question. *"It was too dear"*.

Isobella sold all the furniture she could. It was a case of bare necessities, a table, some chairs and a multi-coloured home-made hooked rag rug in front of the fire range. A few knives, forks and spoons, plates and mugs and pans remained in the kitchen. Huge picture frames, filled with ornate funeral cards were hung upon the walls. When there was a death 'funeral cards' were printed and sent to relatives and distant friends. Isobella said the cards were so pretty that it was a waste not to use them .

"Huge picture frames filled with ornate funeral cards too pretty to waste."

A sad tale from nearby Stalybridge 1901 and more funeral cards.

In Affectionate Remembrance of
JOHN NORTON,
Son of James and Mary Ann Norton,

Who departed this life June 25th, 1875.
AGED 9 MONTHS.

And was interred at the Primitive Methodist Chapel, Waterside, June 27th.

It seemed so hard to let him go, | Soon shall we join our loved one, where
Our brightest beam of joy below; | No sorrow comes, no dark despair;
But he has gone to that blest place, | Till we give him back to him,
Where he beholds our Father's face. | Who took him from this world of sin.

CALEB WARHURST,   UNDERTAKER.

In Remembrance of
Samuel Dearnaley
Who died on the 10th Instant in the 80th year
of his age and was interred
at Woodhead Chapel
September 15th 1863

Sketch of old Hadfield Hall
in the original village of Hadfield

J Killeen

"A glimpse of the factory system" was the heading to the report of the inquest at the Pineapple Inn, Stalybridge, on Hannah Marvel, aged six months, who died from natural causes. The parents worked six looms in Cheetham's new mill, earning about 25/- per week. The baby was put out to nurse with a neighbour at five weeks, the mother taking it between five and six each morning. She returned at breakfast and dinner-time to suckle the baby, as she had done with her three previous babies, none of whom lived more than eight months.

"She stayed with it as long as she durst if she was to be at her work on time, and it was two or three minutes before two when she left it." One juryman said there were many married women in Stalybridge who would rather go to the mill than stop at home to nurse their children.

Another said that he had worked in a Lancashire manufacturing town six years and had never seen what might be witnessed any working morning in Stalybridge, namely men going through the streets with cradles in their arms before six o'clock, and women with babies in their arms wrapped in shawls to keep them warm at that early hour.

Life carried on and it seemed that just as she thought things were becoming bearable Isobella was in for a shock. One day a woman from one of the houses in the street asked Maggie to go up to the Palatine Hotel for a pint of beer. She was given a large jug and promised a penny for her trouble. Her mother said not to fetch it but the penny Maggie was offered was too much to resist so she went on her way up the street to the Palatine to fetch the beer. Her mother ran up the street after her to stop her wilful daughter and they had words outside the Palatine Hotel.

Isobella instructed Maggie to take the empty beer jug back which she did with a thunderous face. Maggie was seen coming from the Palatine with a beer jug and her mother was seen with her.

"Someone told the Board of Guardians and Mother was sent for to appear before them. Mother and baby and Maggie walked wearily up over the hill and down into Glossop to appear before the stern and formidable Guardians. They listened to her story and they stopped Isobella's weekly money altogether. No more money for us."

It made no difference when someone with rare courage, spoke up for Isobella and said they could prove that Maggie had not been up to the pub to buy beer for her mother - the Guardians would not change their minds.

The Morse family were back to the bare necessities. Once again Isobella faced life with an unbreakable spirit. They survived on bread, dripping and tea. Left over tea was saved from one brew to the other so that less tea was used and the old left over brew eked out the next. In some poor households, if there was a man in the house with an empty pipe, the exhausted tea leaves were mixed and chopped with dried dock leaves. This concoction provided the man with an extra fill or two for his pipe.

Isobella spent most of her waking hours 'bettying' for other people. This meant doing all manner of mindless dirty domestic jobs for a pittance. Her aim was to return to the mill as soon as her small son Harold could be looked after by a minder.

When the school dinner bell rang, the Morse children would race out of school to the women in the streets who undertook to cook dinners for the cotton operatives, for the chance to carry them to the mill. The operatives stood at the mill gates to receive their dinners. Many of the village children did this task for three pence a week. Sometimes the Morse children were almost overcome by the delicious smell that floated up from the basket but it was more than their lives were worth to take a piece of 'currant fat cake' near the top of the basket. The three pence they received at the end of the week was too important to lose.

When they reached the mill gates the men would come out with their breakfast tins and collect their dinners. The children would sometimes call, *"Any crumbs in your tin Mester?"* If this ploy did not work they would return home to their almost bare larder to mix oatmeal and sugar and put the mixture into a paper bag. With a duly moistened finger, they would dip their finger into the mixture and suck the mixture off. They considered this a treat. Another treat was a bag of sugar bits and then a quick forage for small pieces of raw rhubarb to dip into the sugar.

Maggie's brother Harold used to hurry home with a bag of thick potato peeling from his 'dinner lady'. They would wash the peelings thoroughly and boil them when the fire was lit in the evening. *'Right good'* was the verdict.

The children ran endless errands for a copper or two. They regularly collected old jam jars and took them back to the confectioners' shops for a halfpenny. Sometimes the shop assistant, overcome by the vast quantity of jam jars recovered by the children would give them a vanilla bun or a small apple pie for their trouble instead of the halfpenny reward.

There was a pawnshop on Station Road and the Morse children thought that it was hilariously funny to see many of the mothers take their place early on Monday morning in the long queue to put the family 'best' clothes back into pawn, only to return to redeem them on Saturday so that their family could wear them to Sunday church and Sunday school. The best of it was the Morse family had not got any Sunday clothes so they were saved the indignity of queuing outside the pawnshop - so they told themselves.

They were not entitled to anything from the church 'Poor Fund' for they did not attend Church or Sunday school. The Morse children were considered *'not quite the thing'* because Maggie and her siblings had no 'Sunday best' clothes. They only had clogs, no Sunday best shoes. They were therefore fair game for scorn and insults from other children who did not hesitate to be cruel. But their mothers had a silent sympathy and helped when they could, for *'there but for the Grace of God go I'*.

"Sometimes one of the neighbours would give an old dress or two for us. You wore them even if they were ill-fitting and too long. You had to put up with the remarks from other girls like, 'My Mam gave 'em to your Mam, she was goin' to let the Rag and Bone man 'ave 'em but 'e wouldn' t 'ave em'.

Christmas dinner that year was a few boiled potatoes and bacon bits. Stoically they made the most of a good fire and sang their hearts out with carols.

Most people in Maggie's street never went to bed on Christmas Eve. There was cooking going on all night despite the fact that most of the women had been at work all day. The Church carol singers visited the street and some women would bring out freshly made mince pies for them. The Salvation Army Band sometimes came to the top of the street and the children rushed up with a penny for the collecting box. People were really nice to one another, wishing one another a Happy Christmas.

Someone would make a big meat and potato pie in a large enamel washing up bowl or a rabbit pie and ask some of the neighbours in. They would have supper and sit around the roaring kitchen fire and sing songs and carols throughout Christmas Eve.

The Morse family did not get asked for Isobella told the children that they could not afford to ask folk back. She pointed out that people had enough to say about them when they gave the Morse family their food left overs during the year, they were not going to be able to say what they gave them at Christmas.

"We put our stockings up that Christmas and we got an apple and an orange and a halfpenny sugar mouse.

My sister and I never had a doll, never saw a pantomime and never went to a circus. Still I don't think I am any worse for it. I had other enjoyments."

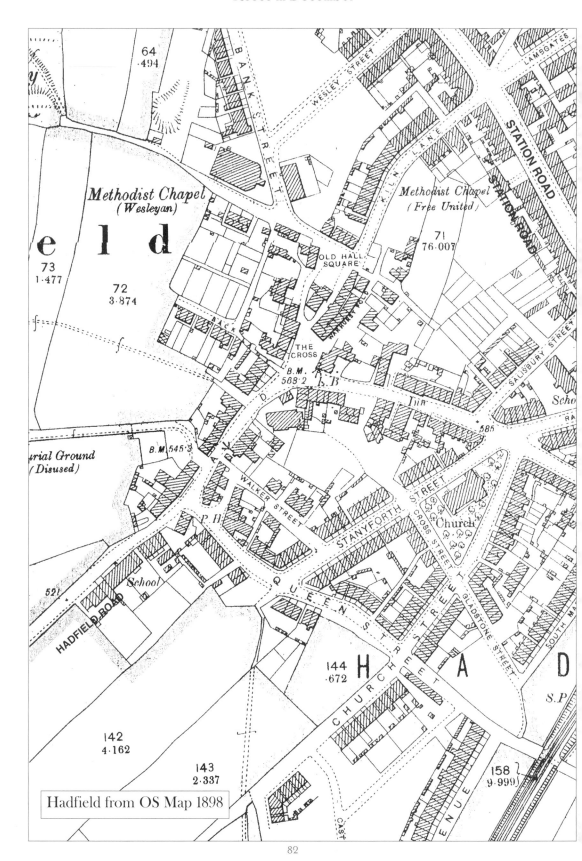

Hadfield from OS Map 1898

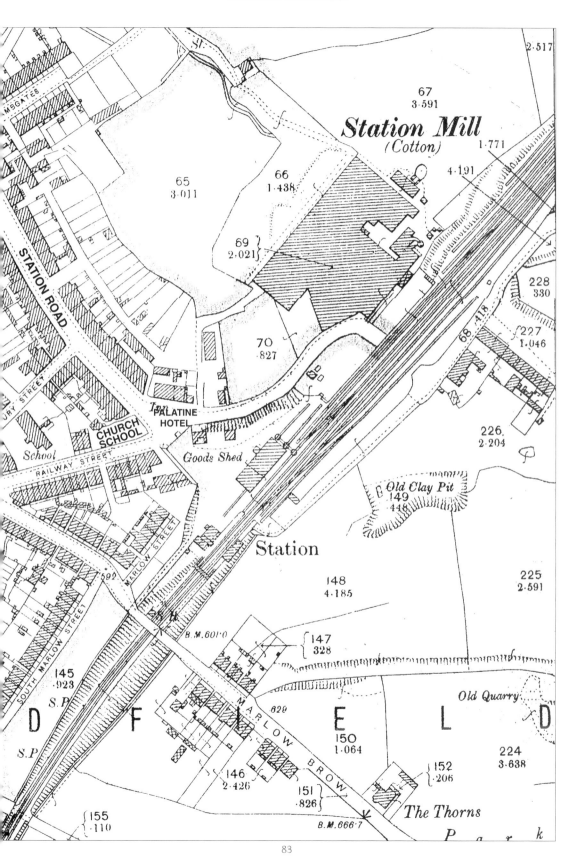

A walkers' paradise to be discovered in Hadfield.

Enjoying a day out at Blackpool.

Six
MAGGIE MORSE
ENJOYS HERSELF

At Easter there was always a day set aside for Stamford Park in Ashton-under -Lyne, seven long miles away, but it was a day out!

You would see mothers with swarms of children setting off to walk to Woolley Bridge, up to Hollingsworth, and then the long puff up Mottram Moor, and along the road to the deep cutting through to the top of Staley Wood. It was a relief to stop half way through 'the Cut' to look up at a white painted stone. It was said that during the work on the cut this stone was knocked into two and out jumped a frog much to the amazement of the workmen.

Next it was a rush to catch a tram down into Ashton where everyone gathered in Stamford Park. Maggie just enjoyed being there. She knew not to ask her mother for a penny for sweets for it was a choice - Stamford Park, or stay at home and have a penny for sweets.

It was lovely at the Park. There were lots of trees and bed upon bed of Spring flowers. There was a bandstand where a local band delighted their audience with stirring popular tunes.

The park featured a boating lake that attracted a few hardy swans. There was also located a big glass and wood conservatory where all sorts of exotic plants from foreign parts had been brought home by learned British botanists.

There was always a procession in Ashton on Easter Monday. It was called 'Riding the Black Lad'. It was held to perpetuate the disgraceful actions of Sir Ralph Ashton, who in 1483 exercised great severity upon the people of that district. A man in a horse-drawn cart, with his face blacked, headed a procession through the town where an effigy made of straw was hung up at a cross in the market place and there 'shot away' in the presence of a large crowd.
The town was packed for this event but Maggie thought it too scary to witness so she stayed in the park.

Even the daunting seven mile walk back to Hadfield was worth it. On some occasions it poured with rain during the entire journey home. When at last they were home, the two sisters lay in bed that night talking about their day out, until slumber stole them away. It was work again tomorrow.

Jim was Maggie's elder brother who was friendly with a young man called Sam. Sam had three allotments 'under the spade' in nearby Platt street, Padfield. That particular summer it occurred to Sam that someone was taking more from the allotments than his family were. He talked about this to his friend Jim Morse and they decided to do something about it.

There was a high wall at the foot of the allotments and this made them decide it must be a male thief. In the corner of the allotments was a partially buried wooden barrel with a sturdy wooden top. They decided that whoever came over the wall used the barrel top as a foothold down into the allotments.

The barrel contained several buckets of horse manure diluted by several buckets of water from the mill owner's brook near by. This foul smelling concoction was stirred regularly and used as liquid feed on the allotments. The boys filled the barrel up to within 6" of the top with stagnant water and Jim found a dead hedgehog and dropped that into the barrel for good measure.

That evening Sam left the barrel lid OFF before they went home. Maggie was let into the plot by Jim, who doted upon his sister - she had him twisted around her little finger. Sam and Jim, with Maggie trailing behind, returned to the allotments early the following morning. Lo and behold, God had looked after his own. The thief had jumped down off the wall onto the barrel lid that was not there, and there were horse dollops splashed around wherever you cared to look. The thief never returned!

At Easter and Whitsuntide, Hadfield and Glossop railway stations were really busy. Hadfield railway station was the last but one stop before Penistone on the Manchester-Sheffield line that ran through the Woodhead tunnel. There would be train loads of passengers from the city smoke and it made Maggie wonder where they all came from.

Most of them were hikers, escaping from the polluted city air of Manchester, bound for the clear uncontaminated air of Doctorsgate, and starting off in Old Glossop. Some of them made for the Derbyshire side of the Longdendale Valley. Many of them just walked down Station Road, turned down Lambgates, strode over the small bridge over the stream and up Roughfields to cross the road and find themselves in the beauty of the reservoirs with their wooded surroundings.

In summertime, every Saturday, Maggie would hear the cries of a hawker with his pony and his two-wheeled flat cart, loaded with salads from Ashton Moss, calling out his arrival. After a tour of Hadfield he did the rounds of neighbouring Padfield. As he turned off Platt Street into Post Street he would stop his pony, wedge a brick under the wheels, put the feed bag on its head and disappear into the Conservative Club on Barber Street for an hour or two.

One boring Saturday afternoon a group of older children, Maggie included, were familiar with the Hawker's progress. When he vanished into the Club, they let him settle and put their plan into action. Maggie stood and watched as the older boys took the pony a little further up Post Street until it was opposite the common yard of a long row of cottages. They unharnessed the pony and took it into the yard then shut the gate. Together they pushed the cart shafts through the five-barred gate and harnessed the pony up again. Now they scattered, to await developments.

Eventually the hawker tottered out of the Conservative Club. He was what is known in local terms as 'well-oiled'! For several minutes he was clearly very puzzled as to how his pony had arrived in the yard with the gate closed, while from a safe distance the spectators thoroughly enjoyed their prank. Sadly they knew that the trick could only be played once.

The Elgy family lived at the corner of Station Road at Osborne Place. The young couple were moving to live in Platt Street, Padfield, so Maggie went to watch the fun. Their 'new' house was across from Rhodes' Hadfield Mills, better known as Top Mill.

Harry Greaves, the coal dealer, who lived in Brickfield Street in Padfield, was to 'flit' the Elgy family. He arrived with his horse and cart, and soon 'Ike', their small two and a half year old son, was placed firmly in the middle of the cart with the family furniture and belongings packed around him. As it was no distance, his mother and father walked ahead into Padfield, with a curious Maggie in tow.

When all the goods and chattels were off the cart, they could not find Ike, so young Mr Elgy had to walk back into Hadfield, searching for his son, and Maggie joined in the search. Eventually Ike was found sitting on the doorstep of his 'minder', Mrs Mitchell, eating a 'jam butty'. Mrs Mitchell lived in Yorkshire Row and she looked after Ike while both his parents worked.

There were many older village women who did this job. They were very long hours, for the children had to be dropped off before 6 o'clock in the morning and were not collected until after 6 pm. Some minders even took very young children to board from Monday morning until Saturday dinnertime.

Things were eased a little for Isobella 's family when Maggie's sister Elsie was 12 years old and allowed to work half-time at the mill. She trained to become a weaver at Waterside Mill. Women cotton workers outnumbered men and when they were trained they could earn 'good money'.

One week Elsie started at 6 o'clock and worked through to 12.30. Then she went to school from 2 pm 'til 4.30 pm. Saturday morning, it was at the mill from 6 o'clock and work through until 1pm. Her pay was three shillings a week.

Later Elsie went into service at Southport for three ladies. There was one less to feed for her mother, and a little money sent home from time to time helped the family. For the time being the ultimate fear of the workhouse, and the terrible disgrace it meant, was lifted.

Maggie knew that there were many children in what was called 'Shire Hill', the Glossop Workhouse. Some of the children were in with their parents or their mothers; worse still some of the mothers were not married. On Sunday mornings some of the inmates went to Glossop Parish church and some to nearby All Saints Catholic Church. *"You could tell who they were because their clothes were different from other people."*

"When the workhouse girls were old enough they were sent out into the world to fend for themselves. The girls were taught housework and lots of them 'went domestic'- domestic service was the biggest single employment for women. The workhouse kitted them out with a basic wardrobe."

Maggie thought their wages were about ten shillings a month and they had to pay for their own uniform clothes and shoes. *"Poor little blighters slept in the attic, up about three flights of stairs. In winter they had to break the ice in the water jug before they could put the water in the bowl for a wash. As for going to the 'lavy', the chamber pot under the bed was for emergencies only, they were told firmly so they had to hang on until they could go downstairs to the outside 'lavy' the staff used.*

These poor girls had to clean all the fire places out and light the kitchen range before 6 o'clock in the morning, and after that scrub the kitchen table."

Maggie felt so thankful that she wasn't one of those poor souls. *"They didn't get much time for pleasure but in spite of the hard life of domestic discipline they led when they were young, most of them made jolly good citizens. One of the workhouse boys became an Alderman on Glossop Council and he was not ashamed to say where he was brought up."*

It was the old people that Maggie felt sorry for. Some of them had no other option but the workhouse. In 1908 the elderly were granted an old age pension of 5/-a week for single women. It was 7/6d for married couples. They had to wait until they were 70 before they could apply. After the regular hazards of childbirth, followed by the menopause, most of the women were old and work-weary before they were 50! It was not long then before they donned the bonnet and shawl and became old women.

Hard living conditions, combined with a harsh climate and a poor diet, did not provide for a good old age. Unable to work, the money was scarce and the spirit of fight had long since been worn away by misfortune, not always of their own making. Grown up children were not always able to help their parents financially, especially if work was scarce, and it wasn't always possible for an overcrowded household to take in ageing parents.

"I'll end up in the workhouse" was a dread that was part of the lives of many old people, and the inevitable pauper's funeral unless someone in the family had insured them. At some workhouses, the coffin was put on a handcart and taken up to the common pauper grave at the cemetery.

When the Morse family eventually possessed the passport to respectability, a pair of shoes for Sundays, there was the Christmas party for the Sunday school to look forward to: *"You got a right good blow-out. A lot of the other children used to do their party piece but not me. There were humourous sketches like, 'Clothes Mangled Here' or a Cornet solo. Some people gave recitations like, 'Trouble in Amen Corner' or a dialogue entitled 'Irish Servants'. If someone stood up and started to recite, 'The boy stood on the burning deck', we would whisper 'with a string of sausages round his neck'. I used to like to laugh with the others - but not make a fool of myself publicly.*

We had to listen to the Parson give his address, and sing the hymn, 'Come thou font of every blessing' before we all stood to attention to sing the National Anthem. Every child received an orange as they departed for home.

When we were young that was the only extra pleasure we had at Christmas."

They paid for this pleasure dearly for Isobella insisted that they attend Church and Sunday school every week. Maggie said her mother would have 'clouted' her children if she knew what they got up to in Church; *"When the congregation said the Lord's Prayer we used to say 'Our Father who art in Heaven' - then we continued - 'If we can' t be there for six, we' ll be there for seven'. Instead of singing 'Here I stand with one plea' we would sing 'Here I stand without one flea'."*

Every year there was a Diocesan Scripture Inspection by an appointed clergyman that created tension within the school. The school was given a time and a day - that was a change from the Government School Inspector who arrived unannounced to test the General Knowledge of the pupils. One of these ogres asked Maggie who was her favourite politician. She answered with the first name that came into her frozen mind, *"Kier Hardy, sir"* and they all waited for the bomb to go up, but it didn't. What a relief it was for staff and pupils when they saw the coat tails of these two 'bogey' men disappearing down the road for another year.

Children were rewarded for regular church attendance at a weekly evening service. They received a regular invitation to an evening 'children's treat'. They were given coffee and buns and sweets. There was a talk followed by lantern slides or listening to a gramophone.

This was a real treat, for records of people like the famous singer Nellie Melba cost as much as a guinea each to buy, and of course the Morses didn't have a gramophone. There were records of comic songs as well as popular ballads. Only the well-off could afford such things.

The Annual Sunday School prizegiving took place on a Saturday when the parents could attend. Coffee and buns were served for parents at 4.30 and at 6.30. The Parson gave an address on 'Books and Manners'. There were some lovely books given as prizes for regular attendance, which Maggie and her siblings treasured for many years. There was always some entertainment like a pianoforte solo, a mouth organ solo or a dialogue like 'Rival Relatives'.

The generous local benefactor who had given a large contribution towards the cost of the prizes was heartily applauded by everyone before the National Anthem was sung.

At Christmas there was a 'Sandwich Tea' followed by an entertainment. Sometimes the Hollingworth Bell Ringers would come to entertain them or the Glossop Concertina Band.

Before the Sunday School Summer break the pupils were given a card to give to their parents that gave them seven rules for the children to follow. It asked the parents and family friends to help and observe the little ones during the coming months:

1. A daily prayer
2. Bible reading
3. Being kind,thoughtful and loving at home, school and play
4. Being bright and happy, trying to be like Jesus
5. Being clean in their habits
6. Abstaining from all intoxicating liquors
7. Attending the meetings of the Bible Class regularly and punctually.

If the children could incorporate such regulation in their daily living, they would render their lives nobler and better the card stated.

The cotton trade was never stable so where people went for a 'Treat' depended upon the generosity of their benefactors and last year's profits. One year Isobella went with members of the 'Mothers Meeting' on a pleasant outing to the Tollemache Arms on Holme Moss Road, Woodhead, not many miles away. About 40 ladies were conveyed in a waggonette by Mr J Bellfield. The fact that the inn was teetotal did not mar their pleasure. They enjoyed their tea and the party returned home at 8.00 pm.

There were regular donations to the 'Poor Fund' at Church and the names of the donors were printed in the monthly Parish magazine as an encouragement for other donations. Many Church offertories were regularly directed to the 'Poor fund.'

At Easter, the Sunday collection went to the Vicar and a great many of his congregation attended for they knew by this he would receive enough money to pay some of his bills or a modest holiday. At other times the offertory went to the Vicarage Repair Fund.

Maggie's sister Elsie had a fine soprano voice and she sang in the choir at St Andrew's Church in Hadfield. As a thank you to the choir, the poor choir-master had to tramp around the district, cap in hand, asking for donations for the Choir Outing. Elsie went on several Choir Outings to Blackpool and Southport from Hadfield station, all expenses paid. She came home with tales of Blackpool Tower and the three piers to walk along, electric tramcars that ran along the front and outdoor dancing places. Her family hung upon every word of her tales of this wonderland by the sea.

Harvest Festival was a good time, for the Church was decorated with flowers, corn and fruit and vegetables. There were gifts of eggs and jam - all the children took gifts. The church roof was lifted with the sound of the Harvest hymns. Afterwards some of the food was sent to the old people and the needy, and the following day the flowers, jam and eggs were taken up to Glossop Workhouse by the vicar.

In spite of the poverty, life provided Maggie with some hectic moments, such as the time when a man came to the village with a dancing bear. He had the large animal on a long chain that to Maggie's eyes did not look very substantial. The bear looked at Maggie, who was jumping up and down with excitement. Maggie looked at the bear. The bear looked back at Maggie and she flew for her life back home. For a week after that her mother could not fault her behaviour; *"The truth was I was too scared to misbehave, I kept thinking this great lumbering beast would come after me."*

There was always entertainment when the 'tramp weavers' were summoned by the mill. They used to stay in bare mill cottages along Bank Bottom, and there were some characters amongst them. They would not hesitate to throw their 'slops' through the bedroom windows so it was a matter of rushing past the cottages as quickly as possible at certain times of the day! The locals were not always innocent though. It was not unknown to hear a crash of glass as a brick went through one of the few windows left in the tramp weavers' cottages, as a man went home after a night out at the Commercial Inn.

There were the usual 'free for alls'. It amused Maggie that the police never raced to the scene. They seemed to let the contenders fight off their initial rage before they attempted to intervene. Maggie would be there in the front row of spectators. She was always disappointed when the 'Black Maria' arrived to cart off the culprits.

The women tramp weavers used to wear a striped petticoat under a dress skirt. When they were ready to start work they used to take the top skirt off and put on a white calico apron. It was how the name originated - the weavers were always known as 'Poverty Knackers'. You would see them in the village one week and the next they were gone. No-one ever saw them come or go. They had the same pay as the local workforce. They never settled anywhere hence the name 'tramp weavers'.

Another source of interest were the Irishmen who used to come to help with the hay-making. They were called the 'July Barbers' by the local folk, coming in June, and drifting back to Ireland late in September or early October.
"Oh my! The lovely fights that used to take place when they got their pay," Maggie commented. Some of the Irishmen settled and married Hadfield girls.

One superstition Maggie held, when out and about, was meeting anyone with a squint. *"It was dreadful, in fact it was like meeting the Devil himself. It put you into quite a panic."*

Everyone was interested in making a little more money to eke out their earnings. Martin O'Shay who lived in Bankbottom put a card in Tom Bentham's newsagent shop in Station Road, offering to lime wash cellars, loos and kitchens. All colours of whitewashing were done, natural, pink, blue or green. He used to buy coloured ink from Tom's shop to suit the colours that people requested.

A grey whiskered little man called Fred Platt was a very inoffensive and considerate man. He carried a wicker basket filled with needles and pins, safety and straight elastic, and dark mending wool, as well as black and white thread. He walked around Hadfield and Padfield in all weathers plying his trade. If folk could afford it they would always try to buy something from him.

Two brothers called Garlick lived at their father's greengrocer's shop in nearby Bank Bottom. Their names were Hughie and Eustace. Eustace was cruelly nicknamed 'Useless' by many including Maggie who laughed at his antics. He worked at the chip shop at the bottom of Station Road. It was 'Useless' Garlick's job to rise early to peel some of the potatoes before he went to school. One frosty winter's morning when Maggie and her sister were turning the corner by the Commercial Inn, into Station Road, they were bemoaning the fact that nothing ever happened in Hadfield. They saw 'Useless' gingerly navigating his way across the frosty cobbled road with two full buckets of peeled potatoes, when his clogs lost their grip and down he went on to his bottom amidst a hailstorm of potatoes streaming down Station Road.

He sat there for a minute before he was heard to exclaim loudly, *"Oow 'eck"* as he surveyed the scene. When the onlookers had dried their eyes from laughter, a few of them, including Maggie and Elsie, took pity on the boy and gave him a hand to retrieve the dozens of potatoes still rolling in all directions.

On Saturday Eustace Garlick would walk round Hadfield and Padfield with a wicker basket covered with a starched white cloth, selling fried fish from the fish and chip shop.

In Winter Maggie would run up to the coal wharf by Hadfield Station and take one of a stock of small $1/2$ cwt. waggons, filled with coal, for 3d. She would pull it back home and help get the fire going in the coal range for her mother's baking. It was hard work but exciting and fun, now that mother did her own baking again, as each child started working part time. When Isobella made bread, the house was lovely and warm. She always included oven bottom cakes - *"it could be hazardous, as Mother shaped the individual oven bottom cakes you were at risk of being hit with a flying floury piece of dough as you passed by the kitchen table."*

She would sometimes cook a 'blow out' tea, when the family ate hot oven bottom cakes filled with cheese and onion. Another dish Isobella concocted was with sliced potatoes at the bottom then a layer of sliced onions and so on until the dish was filled. When it was nearly done she would remove it from the oven and sprinkle sage and onion stuffing across the top for the last 10 minutes browning in the oven.

"Mother also made potato cakes, with half flour and half mashed potato, binded with a spot of milk and cooked in the oven. The cakes were opened with a knife and a scrape of butter dropped into the middle. They were lovely and filling. Another favourite dish was sliced potatoes and bacon. The sliced potatoes in a dish were barely covered with water, then slices of bacon were placed on top to cook. By the time the potatoes were ready the water had boiled away and the bacon slices were lovely and crisp. Not exotic but very wholesome."

"The butcher used to sell dripping. A slice of home-made bread or hot toast with beef or pork dripping, spread across it with a little of the brown jelly from the bottom of the

dripping jar, finally sprinkled with salt and pepper, had to be tasted to be believed! Another treat was a quarter of brawn from the butcher's between us. It was lovely even on dried bread."

"When Mother baked bread she used to include half a small packet of Epsom salts into the mixture, she said it kept 'us going' - instead of giving us 'opening medicine' once a week. On baking day it did look nice to see bread tins full of bread 'proving' out of the draught in the hearth".

To prepare the coal range for baking was a major operation. Maggie and Elsie got up early to clean the fireplace and prepare the oven. Brushing down the built-up soot from the open chimney with the flue at the top, soon had the girls covered with soot. The next job was raking through the bars that held the 'bass' and removing the ashes from the deep ashpit underneath the grate.

Once the fire was lit there was a bar that dropped down to sit on top the the fire for the frying pan. Another cooking aid was a 'top bar'. This was hooked onto one of the grate basket bars; its purpose was simple, to boil potatoes and vegetables.

Maggie said *"At the end of the operation we used to end up looking like one of the 'Ten Mucky Minstrels'. You never risked setting the chimney on fire for they charged you five pounds a call-out".*

On the right hand side of the grate was a small boiler that you filled with water and the water was warmed from the heat of the fire. On the left side of the fire was the oven. The fire had to be 'got going' well before the oven flue was lifted and the fire coaxed to heat under the oven in order to reach the high temperatures required for bread making. After the bread came out, the pastry went in to cook. Last in the oven was a family hot-pot. Most housewives could control their oven temperature by banking the fire with 'slack' or opening up the fire with a poker that lifted the 'slack' and introduced air.

One week in August was Wakes Week. Every day of week there was a trip somewhere:

Monday.

The workers went either to Oldham or Ashton-under-Lyne.

Tuesday.

Folk mostly stayed within the village, enjoying their freedom. The children searched from early morning for the man who came around with an organ and a monkey on the end of a long rope. The poor monkey would beg for pennies. This exhibition went on from street to street until most of the village had been covered.

Wednesday.

Belle Vue Day. The big day; a trip to Belle Vue Zoo and Pleasure Park, near Manchester.

"You left Glossop station at 9.30 am, armed with a large bag of sandwiches. The fare cost 6d. You got off the train at Ashbury Station and walked the short distance to Belle Vue entrance. The entrance charge was one shilling for the day.

There was a huge zoo to walk around. There was open air dancing. There were roundabouts and a boating lake (if you had the money.)

At night there was a big firework display and people could stay in the grounds as late as 11 pm. Jolly good value for one shilling!"

WESLEYAN

Reform Chapel,

Howard Street, Glossop.

A ❖ Sandwich ❖ Tea

Will be provided in the above place by the Senior
Classes of Young Men and Young Women

On GOOD FRIDAY, APRIL 4th, 1890.

Tea on the tables at 4-30 p.m.

After tea, a Grand Miscellaneous

✳ ENTERTAINMENT ✳

Will be given, presided over by

MR. S. SCHOFIELD.

ACCOMPANISTS—MISS A. TAYLOR AND MR. J. H. SCHOFIELD.

Admission (by Programme) for Tea and Entertainment,

Adults, 9d. each; Children under 12, 6d. each;
Entertainment only, 3d. each

Proceeds to be devoted towards the New School Fund.

"Advertiser" Office, Glossop.

Promise of a treat in store.

✳ PROGRAMME. ✳

HYMN.   PRAYER.   CHAIRMAN'S ADDRESS.

GLEE.............................' Love and Mirth "...........................CHOIR
SONG.......................... " The Tar's Home "............MR. J. BOWDEN
RECITATION...MISS D. WOOD
SONG.................... " The Cricket on the Hearth "......MISS A. WARD
READING.................... " The New Shirt "......MR. J. H. SCHOFIELD
DUET......." Mind you inform your Father "...MR. AND MRS. BENNETT
RECITATION........." The New Church Organ " ...MR. A. SCHOFIELD
SONG........................ " Rose of Alandale " ... .MISS M. WRIGHT
ADDRESS............. ....REV. T. BROMAGE.
GLEE...................... " With Laugh and Song " ....CHOIR
READING..................." Tim's First Speech "............. MR. J. WAIN
DUET..." Larboard Watch "...MESSRS. R. ROBINSON & A. SCHOFIELD
DIALOGUE................. " Wanted a Wife " ....SEVEN PERSONS
PIANO SOLO.. ....MISS A. TAYLOR
RECITATION... " The Sister's Birthday, and the Brother's Gift "......
MISS E. IBBOTSON,
GLEE.................... " Laugh and Grow Fat "..................CHOIR
ADDRESS.. ....MR. J. WAIN.
SONG.............. " Hurrah for the wind and rain "...MR. R. ROBINSON
DUET............................. " A.B.C "...MR. K. OGDEN & MISS WARD
RECITATION........ " The Model Church " ...MR. J. H. SCHOFIELD
SONG.. MR. J. BOWDEN
DIALOGUE........." Wanted a Confidential Clerk "........SIX PERSONS
GLEE .... " When the moon is brightly glowing " ...., CHOIR
DOXOLOGY.

Thursday.

This day was used to catch up on the house work.

Friday.

The big market day at Glossop, three miles away. You could get some real bargains from china to groceries. Other folk stayed at home and had visitors or visited friends.

Anyone who did go to Blackpool for the week paid £5 for their rooms. They bought their own food and the landlady cooked it for them. People were considered to be 'well off' if they went away like this.

"There used to be the Sunday school treats and the Co-op gala. These were held on a Saturday. We used to parade from Sunday School down Station Road and around Hadfield Road, to a field near Mersey Bank House, that Mr Edward Platt let the parson have for the occasion.

We had games and then we had a mug of tea and a bun or two. After a little rest the band would play for dancing from 4 o'clock to 11 o'clock. The field we used was a hay field, after the hay had been gathered in. It gave up a gorgeous smell."

At the Coronation celebrations in 1911 of King George and Queen Mary, Mrs Edward Platt of Mersey Bank House, Hadfield, opened the grounds of their home for a 'Grand Garden Party'. Alas, this was not for the hoy poloy. The guests had their photographs taken outside the house. The gracious hostess was the wife of Edward Platt who inherited Station Mill, Hadfield, as well as mills in Padfield, from his father and uncle.

Maggie started part-time at the mill, like her sister Elsie before her, when she was 12 years old. She had to take her birth certificate and a doctor came to school to examine her before she was allowed to work. The struggle to 'manage' eased a little now. She was paid one shilling and ten pence a week to learn her trade. When she was working full-time her pay went up to three shillings and two pence.

She was allowed sixpence a week to spend. Maggie joined a 'Christmas Club' at the Bank Street sweet and tobacconist's shop. She paid a penny a week towards a shilling chocolate selection box at Christmas. *"Sometimes you were more venturesome and paid one and a half pennies a week for a one and six pence selection box. When you went for it on Christmas Eve you would compare them with the others being handed out and you swore blind that for a shilling, yours was better value."*

There was a Music Hall at Woolley Bridge that provided good entertainment and you could lose yourself there for a couple of hours. Some weeks were devoted to dramas. Other weeks were solely variety, when ten popular songs were sung at every performance. Famous artistes like Marie Lloyd, Dan Leno and Marie Kendal visited in their decline. Maggie always sat downstairs at Woolley Bridge - at the theatre in Glossop she could only afford the gallery or 'the cough and spit' as it was called. She preferred Woolley Bridge. But it had one drawback for Maggie, she was only 4' 11" tall. *"The women wore those big Cartwheel hats and sometimes 3 couples would want to sit together. I was only small and it used to annoy me if I had to sit behind them because I couldn't see. If I saw some group approaching I used to dodge on to another seat so that they were divided and I was plonk in the middle.*

Waiting to go for a treat.

Waiting for a train on Glossop Station.

Sometimes they would give me 6d to go and sit elsewhere and that was fine for me because it meant I could go again on another night. It was fine until someone told Mother and that put a stop to my little side-line. Theatres used to send their advertising bills to the local shops for display. If you could acquire a bill you got into the theatre free of charge. You felt one of the privileged few!

I remember one night in particular, it was a melodrama. It was the usual plot about the betrayed daughter and the wicked Squire. It just got to the part where the daughter was told never to darken her father's door again and take her brat with her. Of course the villain had been knocked down and the old father hoped or thought that he lay senseless on the floor. As the daughter was going out of the door, up pops the villain to swipe the old man from behind! Suddenly a voice in the audience in broad dialect yelled out, "Look out e's baun' ter 'it thee!" You can imagine the great laugh that went up and the curtain came down in a hurry.

For 6d you had a real good night out. If the weather was bad you went down to Woolley Bridge on the tram for a half penny. Entrance was three pence and you could dash out in the interval for a halfpenny bag of chips. You had twopence over. You had wealth untold!

The performance used to start at 7.30 to 9 o'clock and from 9 o'clock to 11 pm. You got good value for your money and you got to hear all the popular songs. When you were waiting to go into the Second House you could usually tell whether it was all right because people coming out gave their opinions which were many and varied.

There were some great waggonette outings. They didn't go too far but they would sometimes go to Buxton; or the Cat and Fiddle high up in the hills above Buxton; or they would journey to a pub on the Snake Pass.

Off we folk would go. We were all dressed up in our finery for the day, mostly begged or borrowed. Women were in each other's houses to have their laced whalebone corsets tightened or have their newly feathered hat approved of. Each waggonette was pulled by two horses. Inside the waggonette were two long wooden forms facing one another and upon these forms the travellers sat laughing and joking, their eyes bright with anticipation of the fun day ahead.

All went well 'til it came to a hill and there were quite a few of them on any journey. The men had to get out and push the waggonette up the gradient to a certain point and then it was a case of everybody out - and you all pushed together! It was too much for the horses to pull up the gradient when it was full. It makes you wonder who had the fun! I think myself the horses had the most enjoyment seeing people do their work!

All the pushing and pulling was forgotten though when you reached your destination. You took your food to a large catering hut in a field. There were long wooden scrubbed tables and chairs for folk to sit upon to eat the food that they had brought from home. You contributed a screw of paper that held your tea leaves and sugar to the large communal tea pot provided for the party. Boiling water was supplied to make the tea, and mugs were provided. Most folk took a small brandy bottle filled with milk.

The party re-assembled for the return journey. The horses brought them home at a spanking pace. Voices were raised in harmonious choruses until the distant outline of the mill chimneys in the valley told them that they were homeward bound.

There were other lively times to be had, dancing in the street. Someone would bring out a Melodeon and start to play music for dancing. Gradually the couples would gather and there would be about 20 to 30 couples dancing in the street. Some of the older people would go indoors and make some tea. Another would make some sandwiches and sometimes someone would bring out a cake to share. Everyone found something to contribute - and we used to have a lovely supper. That was one of the nights that Maggie looked forward to. Of course it was proper dancing, not skimming around like a lot of dragonflies."

Maggie and her friends walked over to Glossop every Saturday night to a dance. The village boys used to walk them home and the night was full of laughter and larking about as they made their way over the tops and down into Hadfield.

"In winter there were 'meat and potato suppers' held in church halls. Several women made pies in large enamel washing up bowls and took them up to the venue. Working women would put up the money for a pie to be made. Jars of pickled onions and pickled red cabbage were donated. Every one took their own plate, knife and fork.

Village folk got to know the good cooks so there was always a rush to the table that held the good cooks' pies. Less talented cooks found their pie eaters had to be directed to their tables. A cup of tea was provided. After the meal was consumed, the floor was rubbed with several wax candles to help the dancers. The pianist settled down at the piano with her page turner companion and the dancing commenced."

Maggie was a survivor, but in the late twenties when the Cotton Slump arrived, she almost failed to survive. Eventually she left the mill and went to work at the Norfolk Laundry in Glossop.

"Many souls were condemned to the worst fear of all, the 'Means Test'. You would go to draw the dole and they decided to send someone to interview you. Fair enough, but by the time they had finished you were left both mentally and physically exhausted. They wanted to know all your business. If you had a nice home you were told to sell most of the furniture and live off what you got for it. You were told there was no dole for you.

It was a case of fighting for survival. It was a harsh, cruel and bitter life. Glossop Dale was a real distress area. During the Cotton Slump many mills in the area closed down. Glossop Workhouse was bulging at the seams and men were arriving at the gates demanding admittance.

There were quite a few people who took their own lives, poor things. Life was too hard for them. They had no fight left. When people did kill themselves they were not taken to church, in fact some of the Ministers would not come outside their home to pray for them. They had committed the unforgivable sin of suicide. They were buried in unconsecrated ground along with the vagrants. They had a plain, thin, wooden coffin. The gravediggers lowered the coffin into the ground, and the earth was hastily shovelled over the coffin without any prayers said. It was callous and unchristian.

As regards the 'Nobs' I do not recollect them doing much for the working people. The gap between them was just too big. There were two classes and the ordinary people were kept in their place."

The pub with no beer, the Tollemache Arms, Holme Moss Road.

Cooking facilities for baking days.

Coronation Day Garden Party given by Mrs Edward Platt at her home, Mersey Bank House, Hadfield.

Ruby, in cartwheel hat, the bane of Maggie's
life at the Music Hall.

Arthur and Elizabeth Mary (Polly) Wadsworth, with son George, when they
arrived at the Junction Inn, Mottram.

Seven

LIFE AT THE JUNCTION INN,
MOTTRAM IN LONGDENDALE, 1895

Early print of Mottram in Longdendale

Polly and Arthur Wadsworth moved to Mottram in Longdendale in 1895 to take over the tenancy of the Junction Inn. They had been married for three years and had a small son, George, aged one. There were 24 public houses already in the area so they were not without competition. The Junction Inn held a strategic position at the junction of the four roads that led in and out of the village, to Glossop, Stalybridge and Hyde, and it was on the road from Stockport to Penistone in Yorkshire.

Mottram was a village of some 3,128 people. The Industrial Revolution led to a dramatic increase in the population after the first cotton mill was built in nearby Broadbottam in 1790. Mottram Hill rises above the neighbouring village of Hollingworth to a height of 450 feet and commands magnificent views of the villages beneath and the beginning of the Pennine Range.

Mottram was famous for its Parish Church of St Michael, built in 1478; because of its lofty eminence it was a landmark that could be seen for miles and miles around, and there were tales in the village of the period when body snatchers were at work in the graveyard.

The village had an old grammar school founded in 1612, which had fallen into disuse, but in 1848 the school was restored at a cost of £200 given by a local squire, George Woodhead. Mottram Grammar School had carved over its threshold, 'Manners Maketh Man'.

The Manor House was occupied by the widow of a mill owner, Mrs Sidebottom. John Wagstaffe JP lived at Mottram House. Mr George Wood Rhodes JP, the son of a wealthy mill owner, also had a gracious residence in the village. A mile from the centre was Mottram Old Hall, once the home of the Woodhead family and now in the hands of a Walter Wedgewood.

Lord Tollemache was the principal landowner in the area. Another landowner was Mr E Chapman MA, MP, FLS, who resided in a stone built mansion standing in gracious grounds and called Hill End House, and through his great kindness he helped hundreds of destitute cotton operatives from Mottram, Broadbottom and Hollingworth during the 1862 Cotton Famine. Twice a week the people gathered in the courtyard at Hill End to be given breakfast. In December 1862, *The Illustrated London News* printed a sketch of the cotton operatives waiting for their breakfasts in Mr Chapman's courtyard.

About the same time, the Prime Minister's wife, Mrs Catherine Gladstone, visited a soup kitchen in nearby Ashton-under-Lyne, on a visit to the North to see for herself the woeful plight of the cotton operatives. In one of her letters to her husband she wrote:

"And here the poor things feel they may come in their poor and ragged clothes. There was standing room of about a thousand souls. It was an overwhelming sight to see those sorrowful and pale faces met together in sore trouble."

Mrs Gladstone took several groups of young girls from the area back to her estate in Hawarden, where they were trained for domestic service, and several young men were taken and trained in estate work.

The Great Central Railway had a station one and a half miles from Mottram, in Broadbottom, that provided a more comfortable and faster journey into Manchester, ten miles away, than by road. Glossop, the nearest town, was three miles away.

The Junction Inn was originally a farmhouse built in 1786, along with 35 acres of land, that belonged to the Mottram Estate of Lord Tollemache. In 1822 the Royal Mail coach called at the farmhouse in the afternoon and the 'Norfolk' mail coach from Manchester called every evening on its way to the Norfolk Hotel, Glossop.

New roads were built by the Turnpike Trust and the farm became a Toll Bar in 1826 because of its convenient position at the junction of Market Street, Hyde Road, Stalybridge Road and Mottram Moor. It became known as the Junction Inn in 1836, at which time the buildings were also extended. At the same time a new village smithy was built next to it to catch the coaching and horse traffic that came to the Junction Inn. This could account for its long stone structure near to the road with a square of buildings at the back.

At the back of the Inn, across a large square cobbled courtyard, were stables that housed four horses and a coach house. There were several pig sties and a large hen pen. Leading out of the courtyard was an orchard garden and an established bowling green that was rented along with the Inn from the Tollemache Estate.

Opposite the stables was the main building that began with a curing room complete with the stone slabs for the bacon and big hooks in the ceiling for the hams. To the left of the main entrance was a Tap Room. To the right were the Best room and Family room. There was a corner Snug tucked next to it. Opposite this was a large kitchen, pantry and scullery. Next came the Serving Bar and Snug no 2. Here stood the two cellar doors that led to the beer and wine store, beyond which was the Wash House and out in the yard, the Gents' lavatory.

Two staircases led the way upstairs. One staircase led to a handsome Masonic Room with a cloakroom and water closet. Alongside was a large Club room. The other staircase led to the family living room, four bedrooms and a bathroom and water closet.

The Inn was lit by gas. The kitchen was a very large room. Cooking was done on a big Yorkshire range with a central fire and ovens either side. The range was big enough to take a fish kettle and a variety of other pans. Some years later a gas cooker was added.

Licensing hours were from 6 am until 11 pm. Beer was twopence a pint. Rum was twopence a small glass. During the winter a gallon of hot coffee was made for opening time so that the men on their way to work down the Moor would call and purchase a cup of coffee and a tot of rum - guaranteed to keep out the cold during the walk to work on the raw, winter mornings to the villages below, where the bleach works and textile mills were situated.

Polly was very new to the beer trade. She was extremely nervous of any drunkeness that might arise when her husband took over the Junction, but her fears proved groundless after seeing Arthur and one of his brothers dispose of their first 'drunk'.

Licensing hours on Sundays were from 12 noon until 2pm and 6pm until 10pm. During the hours in between if a man walked or journeyed three miles from his village he was entitled to have a drink at a public house. Sunday afternoons were busy for Arthur, for second division Glossop Football Club made the Junction Inn their meeting point for a drink between licensing hours.

When Polly and Arthur took over the inn in 1895 it was a free house. Two years later, it had a widespread reputation for fine food, entirely due to Polly who determinedly set about becoming a proficient cook, aided by two large volumes of *Elizabeth Acton* and *Cassell's Dictionary of Food*. Within a year of her arrival she was catering for Masonic dinners for a 100 guests.

Their eldest son, George, was three years old when her second son Dion was born on February 11th 1896. He was a delicate child and during the first month he developed jaundice.

Polly placed him in a padded wicker clothes basket and he was carried by his busy mother as she went about her daily tasks. Somehow Polly calmly coped with her many domestic challenges - as she continued to do throughout her life.

Hannah Jane, their first daughter, was born on January 12th 1898. This was a memorable day when the cat gave birth to six kittens and the sow delivered a record number of piglets. Five years later a second daughter, Phyllis Madeline, was born on January 16th 1903.

Public Houses did not have the finest of reputations in that era. They were viewed in some quarters as a sinister web drawing in working men who were encouraged to spend their money on beer when they should be spending their meagre wages feeding their families and paying the rent, instead of buying the 'Demon drink'. There was a high proportion of drunkards among the working class and many households spent more on alcohol than they could afford. A portion of the blame must have been illness, family size and unemployment. Did drinking cause poverty or was poverty a cause of drinking? The pub was a fast way to escape from their miserable circumstances!

Arthur was loathe to allow Polly to set foot in any of the bars. It was not considered a lady's place to be seen in the public part of the Inn. Indeed when women stood gossiping in the road outside a public house and saw a woman of their aquaintance enter a public house, the other women would exclaim, *"We surely won't bother with that low life thing!"*

On one occasion Polly defied Arthur. She was watching from an upstairs window as a wagonette full of men stopped and spilled out into the inn. One youth did not get out and he looked far from well. Despite Arthur's previous threats, Polly rushed through the bar and asked some of the men to help get the youth out of the wagonette and into their living quarters. Despite all their efforts, sadly the youth died in her arms.

Another of her acts of courage was when she heard the sounds of a shying horse. Running out into the cobbled street to investigate she was horrified to see the rider being dragged along the street, his foot caught up in the stirrup iron. Some men were brave enough to stop the horse and Polly did not hesitate to go to the aid of the severely injured rider.

A more amusing incident occurred when a cab came rattling along the village street at a rare pace. The horse came to a confused stop outside the Junction Inn door. Curious to see the occupant, Arthur opened the door of the cab, to see his elder brother Tim, gloriously drunk and struggling to hold upon his lap a baby donkey that he had bought for his small daughter Ellen. Tim was on his way home to Hadfield where he owned a straw and hay business.

Arthur was not very domesticated and rather squeamish. He kept several hens but he was loathe to kill them. Polly fared no better so Arthur left it to one of her brothers to *'do the deed for them'*. Arthur had such a kind heart that whenever a pig was slaughtered he went to Manchester for the day to avoid any aspect of the killing. Polly's brother, Denman, came from Hadfield to do the killing, or her brother Bill who ran The Organ Inn in Hollingworth.

The first time Denman came to do the ghastly deed he decided to play a trick upon his sister. He called her into the barn; *"Poll, come in here a minute and catch hold of that rope will you?"* The trusting Polly having no idea that the killing was imminent walked into the barn just as the killing was taking place. At the sight of the poor pig having its throat and chest slit, Denman's laughter turned to concern as his favourite sister slid into an unconscious heap upon the barn floor. She never meekly obeyed his commands again.

Both Arthur and Polly cured the bacon and hams. Arthur was most particular about the exact amount of salt petre being used, which he usually inserted into a drilled hole in the bone.

As well as plenty of daily help, Polly engaged a living-in maid called Cissy Possell. Unfortunately, Cissy started sending parcels of food home to her family. At first Polly chose to ignore this practice but Cissy became too greedy and Polly regretfully had to sack her.

When little Mary Lomas arrived on the scene, Polly's troubles were over. Mary stayed with her for over 52 years. She came to Polly when she was 13 years old. She had been working for a year as a general maid in a mens' boarding house in Glossop, where her bed was a blanket on the floor of the mens' 'bathroom'. Her food was the scraps that the men left on their plates after their meals. Mary was a poor underfed little thing who had rarely had clean clothes to change into. She was given clothes from time to time and she wore them until they were in rags or until other clothes were given to her. She had no idea that underclothes were to be changed or even removed for sleeping.

She gazed with grateful wonderment when Polly introduced her to a regular warm soapy bath and provided her with a set of new clothes complete with a change of underclothes. Polly raised Mary's pay to four shillings a week. The kindness Mary was shown was repaid throughout the fifty years she spent with the family. Eventually Mary retired and she was visited regularly by the Wadsworth family. When Phyllis, Polly's second daughter called to see her, Mary would announce to all the company present, pointing to Phyllis, that she had 'brought her up'. They were constant companions during Phyllis's childhood.

The Junction was busy throughout the year. Sometimes the Coroner would ride out to the Inn to hold Enquiries:

"Last Friday afternoon Mr Francis Newton the Coroner of the Stockport district conducted an enquiry at the Junction Inn re Mr W Booth of 'Rose Villa', Mottram Moor".

Before the enquiry commenced Mr Newton would take lunch at the inn which he would heartily enjoy before getting on with the more depressing side of his occupation.

Occasionally they had guests to stay, who were recommended to the Junction. For several years a visiting Dutch actor, turned quick-change artist, came to stay for a week during his annual engagement at a Hyde theatre. He was accompanied by his elegant wife and mother. They became great friends and the annual visit of the Baumeesters was looked forward to with pleasure by Polly and Arthur.

From January 1904 Arthur organised a 'Trail Hunt' that ended near the Junction. There were usually eight greyhounds running, including a champion, 'Mottram Cracker' owned by Arthur. They usually followed a course from the Black Bull's Head Inn at Charlesworth up to the heights of Werneth Low Hill and back down again and across to Mottram Showground, making it a round trail. The man with a specially soaked aniseed rag to give the dogs a scent, left half an hour before the dogs, to set the trail for the dogs to follow. The event was celebrated with a Trail Hunt Dinner at the Inn held upstairs in the large Club room.

Another January event was the Carters' Supper. One held on January 12th 1900 was reported in *the Glossop Chronicle;*

"Last Friday evening at the Junction Inn the Carters of Mottram and Hollingworth held their annual dinner and convivial gathering, the cost of which was kindly subscribed to by tradesmen and others in the neighbourhood.

Host and Hostess Wadsworth placed a capital spread before the company comprising all the seasonable dishes and it is superfluous to state that the excellent viands were soon made beautifully less and the inner man thoroughly gratified".

The Junction Inn became a regular meeting spot for many social groups active in the village. Polly and Arthur hosted some splendid repasts for the Oddfellows Lodges, the Trail Hunt Society and the Mottram Cattle Club. Arthur acted as one of the Club Judges; being a Farmer's son he had a good eye for cattle. The Mottram Harriers met regularly at the Inn.

During the annual Wakes Week the Inn was very busy. There was not much 'going away' or 'going off' to seaside places for the majority of the village folk. Most people celebrated the holiday in their own homes with visiting relatives and friends from a distance. Food was plentiful that week.

The ritual was that every home was cleaned from top to bottom and the kitchen whitewashed ready for Wakes Week Saturday. In Broadbottom, one millowner had all his mill cottages whitewashed throughout, once a year, coming up to Wakes Week. If the tenants were lucky they could ask the workmen to colour the bucket of whitewash with either blue or red ink to make a change from white.

Mottram Showground was famous throughout the area. It held many functions throughout the year and always attracted large crowds. There were two major Cattle Shows a year and an annual Floral, Fruit and Vegetable Show.

The Wakes Fair arrived at Mottram for Wakes Week Saturday and folk came from miles around to take part in the fun. The first Wakes Fair was held in 1799 and had continued throughout the years. You could watch brandy snaps being cooked at one stall. Another stall sold sliced black puddings with streaks of mustard spread on top. There was what looked like a small steam engine that produced baked potatoes.

The judges at Mottram Cattle Show. Arthur is on far left of group.

A Mottram Show enthusiast. Dr William Bowden (centre) surveys the scene.

Mottram Show officials.

Coconuts were two pence each or a slice would cost a penny. It cost two farthings to ride on a set of the latest steam horses, called locally 'dobby horses'. Folk could be swung high above the showground in the 'flying boats'. There were shooting galleries and a photographer's tent to capture you having fun, if you stayed still long enough. There was a 'Bazaar' full of cheap and cheerful objects, not to be found in Mottram.

There was a 'Fat Lady' to stare at, who boasted a hip measurement of 74 inches, beating Queen Victoria by 20 inches! Another equally large woman, encased in a large white apron, sold brooms for children and stranded silks attached to the end of a stick. She would call out *"Who will buy a Bi're broom, one for the children and one for the lady?"*

Mr Herbert Rhodes, a mill owner, used to bring to the village a challenging cricket team to play the Mottram team. The annual match took place on the Monday of Wakes Week. After the match, Mr Rhodes, the officials and both the teams retired to the Junction Inn where a 'Cricket Tea' was waiting. Here they participated in bread and butter, beef, ham, tongue, pickles etc, followed by a fresh fruit salad, sponge cakes and a large fruit cake. And after tea there would follow a sing-song before the satisfied guests departed. Local people said that the Mottram cricket team could always beat the challenging team at eating even if they did not always beat them at cricket!

Mr Rhodes paid the bill and the waiters always enjoyed the 'Cricket Tea' for they all received a 3 shillings and sixpence tip from the generous mill owner.

There was a Wakes' Trail Hunt when dogs from all over the area would come to compete. This trail ran to Bower Fold over the top to Harrop Edge and down again into the village, coming from the other side of the Broadbottom road and across the cricket field before crossing the road back to the famed Mottram showground and the finish. Quite a lot of hard earned money changed hands during this event. It was made an even bigger gamble by the behaviour of the crowd gathered to watch. The dogs lined up for the start, which was usually most orderly. Off went the dogs, with the yells of their supporters aiding them on their way. The 'Finish' was roped off ready but as soon as the returning dogs were sighted crossing the cricket field and approaching the home stretch, some of the excited spectators would make one mad rush towards the competing dogs. In the resulting chaos some of the dogs voluntarily retired and other dogs became lost in the welcoming crowd.

The winner was usually the dog who was not averse to noisy crowds. On one occasion, Arthur's dog, 'Mottram Cracker', disgraced himself by returning home to the Inn and failing to finish the race. His proud trainer, Mr T Sidebottom, could not understand why the dog had not finished the race. Locally it became quite a joke when it was found out that the dog had returned home. Arthur failed to see the joke! 'Mottram Cracker' did go on to win several copper kettles and other prizes elsewhere but he never won the Wakes' Trail Hunt.

Other so-called sports took place on the Showground during the week. There was rabbit coursing with thirty wild rabbits and whippets. The rabbits were sent from Wales to the Junction Inn on Friday and were kept loose in the stables so that they could run about. On the Saturday morning they were sent to the sports field. The sport took the form of two dogs to chase and kill one rabbit. This sport supported a great deal of betting, as did the more horrifying chase between rats and fox terriers, called rat coursing. This took place in a large field behind the Junction some weeks before Wakes Week. Arthur used to send for the

Followers of the Trail Hunt.

Waiting for the Hunt to start at Hill End House, Mottram.

ratcatcher to clear the stables, coachhouse and barn ready for the event on Saturday.

The ratcatcher would bring his ferrets and nets and set about his business, surrounded by a crowd of fascinated youngsters, Dion included, who watched the scary routine. The rats would dash out into the nets and Dion would help to pick up the rats and put them into a sack. Alas, on one occasion a ferret jumped up at the sack of rats that Dion was holding. The terryfiying squeals of the rats so shocked him that he never had any more to do with it.

The pièce de résistance, a most revolting entertainment, was given by a man who travelled the country and came in Wakes Week to give 'exhibitions' with rats. He would arrive at the Junction Inn and asked Arthur if he could clear the stables and barn of rats. The following day he would give his exhibition to a horrified yet fascinated crowd gathered for the fun in one of the Inn's rooms. He would put two rats in a bag and have his hands tied. Someone would open the bag in front of him and the man would put his head into the bag and remove the rats with his teeth. If he could persuade a woman to sit and have a rat on her lap, he would lull it to sleep before the crowd. He had with him a trained dog who would catch or kill any rat according to his master's clap of his hand.

In August the grouse shooting season began on the nearby heather-clad moors. The head gamekeeper was up every day by dawn. It was his big day; throughout the year he had nurtured the grouse on the moors and he knew how many birds there were and their condition.

At 8am the 'beaters' and 'flankers' were ready with their flags to whistle and call to help drive the grouse across the moor and over the guns. One enthusiastic beater was heard to call out loudly "a lord pheasant mi' cock!" much to the amusement of his companions.

Every gun had two Loaders, one to receive the emptied gun and one to hand back the reloaded gun. The 'pickers up' and retrievers were ready to collect up to 1,000 birds a day.

Some of the shooting party arrived by train and were taken up to the moors to the gamekeeper's house, half a mile from the butts. The party drew lots for their positions, the centre being the favourite.

Arthur took the liquid refreshment for the shooting parties made up of influential councillors and aldermen and their VIP business friends from Manchester who used the grouse moors by kind permission of the Manchester Corporation Waterworks.

There was whisky and bottled beer for the shooters and small barrels of ale for the beaters. Arthur, in the pony and trap, took the liquid refreshment up to the gamekeeper's house. He returned later with large padded baskets of food prepared in the Junction's kitchens. There was hot soup and raised pies or standing pies, the hot water pastry made with dripping or chicken fat. Fruit cakes were sent and other substantial dishes. There was fresh bread and cheese for the beaters and lesser mortals who helped to make the day a success.

At lunchtime the gamekeeper and his wife took the food and drinks up to the shooting cabin upon the moors.

There was a large, isolated and grand house between Hollingworth and Tintwistle called The Towers. It was originally built for the Chief Engineer of the Waterworks. It had spacious grounds and a large sheltered kitchen garden. The building was now used for entertaining the VIPs, complete with a resident housekeeper called Mrs Foulks who presided over a small staff. Here the VIPs received further sustinence, shelter and rest.

Excellent fishing facilities were to be had for a superb fishery was incorporated in the land belonging to Manchester Corporation Waterworks.

In May and October the Junction Inn catered for a 'Rent Dinner'.

"October 8th Rent Dinner. The half-yearly dinner of the tenants of the Tollemache Estate was held at the Junction Inn, Mottram on Wednesday. Mr Cawley, representing Lord Tollemache was present."

Mr Cawley was Lord Tollemache's Agent. He stayed overnight at the Junction. The following day he received the tithe rents from the tenant farmers and other tenants, and a meal was provided for the tenants and paid for by Lord Tollemache. After the tenant had paid his rent he was invited to partake of the meal before starting out on his journey back to his land or farm. Sometimes the festivities would continue long into the night.

Lord Tollemache owned most of the land along the Longdendale valley before it was bought by Manchester Corporation to develop a water supply to thirsty Manchester and Salford, after which, every summer, trips were arranged for the citizens of Manchester and Salford to come and see for themselves where their precious water supply came from.

October was the time for the Junction Inn Bowling Green and Games Supper. The Bowling Green at the Junction was Arthur's pride and joy and he became an expert player. He founded the Mottram Bowling Club soon after he arrived in Mottram. They met regularly and held many tournaments. To quote from the newspaper:

"In the evening the teams sat down to a most appreciable supper repast consisting of roast beef, roast mutton, boiled mutton, roast pork followed by plum pudding and pies. A vote of thanks was given from the Chairman and Vice Chairman to their Host and Hostess for their catering".

Gamekeepers and helpers surveying the 'bag'.

There was always a large Bonfire on the 5th of November in the courtyard at the back of the Inn. It was a grand affair and many of the village children came along. Mountains of treacle toffee and parkin were provided, and potatoes in their jackets, half wrapped in paper, partly peeled, smoothed with glistening butter and eaten with a teaspoon.

In December it was the event of the year at the Junction. The Masonic Festival at Mottram of the lodge 320 of Loyalty, Cheshire province. One menu was:

Hare and Oxtail Soups
Cod with Oyster Sauce
Turbot and Lobster
Roast Beef and Boiled Mutton,Caper Sauce
Roast Turkey
Roast Duck and Geese
Boiled and Roast Chickens
Plum Pudding
Marmalade and Bakewell Puddings
Mince Pies
Wine Jellies, Tartlets, Custards
Cheese and Celery
Dessert

The preparations took over a week. The menu was decided upon, approved and then collected from the printers. Extra help was arranged for the kitchen. Provisions were noted and ordered. Upstairs the large dining room was given an extra special clean until the dark mahogany and oak furniture gleamed. The floral decorations were finalised and the flowers ordered. The large white damask cloths and napkins were scrutinised, washed and starched by Mrs Dearnley in the kitchen into the desired three screen folds. Mrs Bevan washed the china and polished the glasses. Mary was busy on the knife machine aided by Oakey's knife powder. The rest of the cutlery was inspected and polished.

Arthur inspected his wine cellar to check that the best wines were plentiful. He had a day in Manchester to buy some of the food. Polly drove him in the pony and trap to the railway station in Broadbottom to catch the early train into Manchester. Once in the city he would command a cab for his many errands. The first to Shudehill Market where Arthur purchased the turkeys and geese, lobsters and fish. Arthur would now adjourn to Yates Wine Lodge in Oldham Street for some sustaining liquid refreshment.

Later clutching his purchases he directed the cab to The Shambles at the bottom of Market Street where he bought special cheeses and other delicacies. He acquired a damp bag of oysters to add to his purchases. His next stop was into St Anne's Square to search for something special for Polly and the children, and then - after a further respite for more liquid refreshment - Arthur was taken back to London Road Railway Station.

Firmly assisted by the cabby, who was of course most suitably rewarded, Arthur and his packages were handed over to a station porter, who loaded him, complete with his purchases, into a compartment on the Glossop train.

During the journey he dozed until the train pulled to a squeaky halt at Broadbottom station. The shouts of the station staff would awaken him and the cold fresh country air would greet Arthur as he opened the carriage door, a welcome change after the smoke of the city.

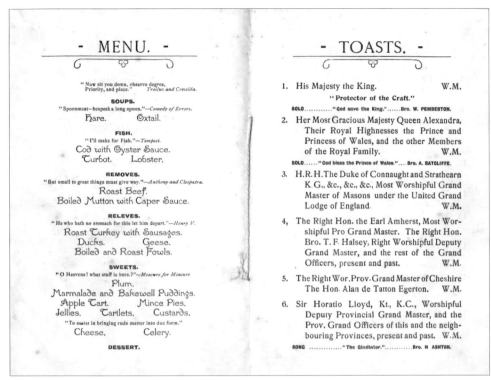

- MENU. -

" Now sit you down, observe degree,
Priority, and place." *Troilus and Cressida.*

SOUPS.
" Spoonmeat—bespeak a long spoon."—*Comedy of Errors.*

Hare.　　　　Oxtail.

FISH.
" I'll make for Fish."—*Tempest.*

Cod with Oyster Sauce.
Turbot.　　Lobster.

REMOVES.
"But small to great things must give way."—*Anthony and Cleopatra.*

Roast Beef.
Boiled Mutton with Caper Sauce.

RELEVES.
"He who hath no stomach for this let him depart."—*Henry V.*

Roast Turkey with Sausages.
Ducks.　　　Geese.
Boiled and Roast Fowls.

SWEETS.
" O Heavens! what stuff is here.?"—*Measure for Measure*

Plum.
Marmalade and Bakewell Puddings.
Apple Tart.　　Mince Pies.
Jellies.　　Tartlets.　　Custards.

" To assist in bringing rude matter into due form."

Cheese.　　　Celery.

DESSERT.

- TOASTS. -

1.　His Majesty the King.　　　　　W.M.
" Protector of the Craft."
SOLO............."God save the King.".....Bro. W. PEMBERTON.

2.　Her Most Gracious Majesty Queen Alexandra, Their Royal Highnesses the Prince and Princess of Wales, and the other Members of the Royal Family.　　　W.M.
SOLO......"God bless the Prince of Wales."...Bro. A. RATCLIFFE.

3.　H.R.H.The Duke of Connaught and Strathearn K.G., &c., &c., &c., Most Worshipful Grand Master of Masons under the United Grand Lodge of England.　　　W.M.

4,　The Right Hon. the Earl Amherst, Most Worshipful Pro Grand Master. The Right Hon. Bro. T. F. Halsey, Right Worshipful Deputy Grand Master, and the rest of the Grand Officers, present and past.　　W.M.

5.　The Right Wor.Prov.Grand Master of Cheshire The Hon. Alan de Tatton Egerton.　W.M.

6.　Sir Horatio Lloyd, Kt., K.C., Worshipful Deputy Provincial Grand Master, and the Prov. Grand Officers of this and the neighbouring Provinces, present and past. W.M.

SONG ...." The Gladiator."...........Bro. H ASHTON.

A porter would unload Arthur and his parcels onto the platform, take his ticket and turn him in the direction of the exit where Polly was waiting in the gathering dusk with the pony and trap. Soon, home in the welcoming warmth and appetizing smells of the Inn kitchen, he would sit munching a newly baked barm cake and a piece of fried undercut steak, while the children eagerly waited to see what their father had brought back from Manchester.

Among the presents was usually a piece of jewellery for Polly to wear at the dinner; a silver and tortoiseshell evening belt or a pair of long jet earrings; maybe a delicate amber brooch, or a pair of long gold decorated earrings. Sometimes it was a pretty silver brooch watch with blue enamel stars on the back, perhaps a heavy gold extending bracelet decorated with turquoise and pearls. It was always bought with the thought that it would give his adored Polly real pleasure and meet with her approval.

The following day the fowls were plucked, scalded and drawn. The leverets were skinned and jointed. Jellies were made and left to set. The pastry making, a gargantuan task for a hundred guests, was made into tartlets and mince pies by Mrs Bevan, who always came for these occasions. The puddings were put to boil for a few hours and the stockpot was at its busiest during the last two days being added to and re-boiled each day. The beef and mutton were prepared for roasting.

Mr Forshaw, a professional waiter, and his team, were engaged to do the 'waiting on'. When Dion was twelve he was allowed to help with the waiting under the eagle eye of his friend, Mr Forshaw. Dion wore a white shirt, a black bow tie and short black trousers, and he held a white folded napkin over his arm with great pride.

The table laying was supervised by Polly. The central fold of the white starched tablecloth ran down the centre of the table exactly. Two candelabras were placed either side, at equal distances from the centre and edges of the table. Polly took care never to overload the table with heavily scented flowers, usually choosing one delicately coloured arrangement in the centre. She checked that all the 'covers' were laid one inch from the table's edge, complete with a dinner napkin folded in a three screen fold placed at the side of each cover.

Finally the day of the banquet arrived. The responsibility of serving a perfectly prepared banquet, without any obvious hitches, to a room full of gentlemen who were used to the very best of food, filled Polly with trepidation. So much so that she usually developed a raging headache and would retire for an hour to lie down before rejoining her helpers in the final hours of preparation.

Polly never minded the hard work and would turn her hand to anything to make sure that everything ran as smoothly as possible, for financially it was most rewarding. She would change into her evening dress and let the children come to admire their elegant mother before she placed a small black waist apron over her finery and began to carve the meat and poultry. Arthur did carve on these occasions but he preferred Polly to start him off.

The last thing she did was to walk round and supervise the last of the decorating and garnishing of the dishes. She would check all the tureens before she calmly walked up the stairs to the Assembly Room to play hostess.

"Wednesday December 8th
The Annual Banquet subsequently took place and was largely attended. An excellent repast was served by the Host and Hostess of the 'Junction Inn' which added to their reputation.

The Toast followed; 'The Royal Family' followed by a Solo. The National Anthem by Brother W Pemberton. Further Toasts, H.R.H. The Duke of Connaught, Most Worshipful Grand Master of Masons under the United Grand Lodge of England was proposed by the Worshipful Master of the Lodge. Finally Sir Horatio Lloyd KTKC was toasted before Brother H. Ashton sang a Solo, 'The Gladiator'.

The various Toasts were suitably acknowledged and the songs by the Brethren made up a very harmonious evening."

There was little time to bask in glory after a successful evening for the Inn doors had to be opened the following morning at 6am.

Schoolmaster's House, Mottram where
the pupils went for lunch.

LOT 1.

(No. 75, and Coloured Brown on Plan.)

ALL THAT VALUABLE FULLY-LICENSED PUBLIC-HOUSE

KNOWN AS

THE JUNCTION INN

occupying an important position at the junction of Market Street, Hyde Road, Stalybridge Road, and Mottram Moor, Mottram.

THE ACCOMMODATION comprises : Two Smoke Rooms, Bar, Snug, Corner Snug, Pantry, Kitchen and Scullery combined, Cellars, Larder, Stable, Coach House. Upstairs is A LARGE CLUB ROOM, 37ft. by 25ft., a HANDSOME MASONIC ROOM, Bathroom, W.C., three Bedrooms, and Box Room.

Also : OUTBUILDINGS AND BUILDER'S YARD at rear, together with the welllaid BOWLING GREEN adjoining, the whole containing are area of about

3 Roods, 16 Poles.

Let on Yearly Tenancies as follows : Public House and Bowling Green, MR. R. SANDIFORD; Builder's Yard, TOLLEMACHE TRUSTEES.

SCHEDULE.

ORD. NOS	DESCRIPTION.					A.	R.	P.
139 Pt....	Public House and Premises	...	...	...		0	2	6
122 Pt....	Bowling Green	...	...	...	...	0	1	10
						0	**3**	**16**

NOTE.—A Public Urinal is erected on part of this site.

Apportioned Tithe Rent Charge : 4s. 6d.

The Towers in snow. It offered hospitality on behalf of Manchester Corporation Waterworks to shooting parties and a spot of fishing to wealthy and influential business men from Manchester.

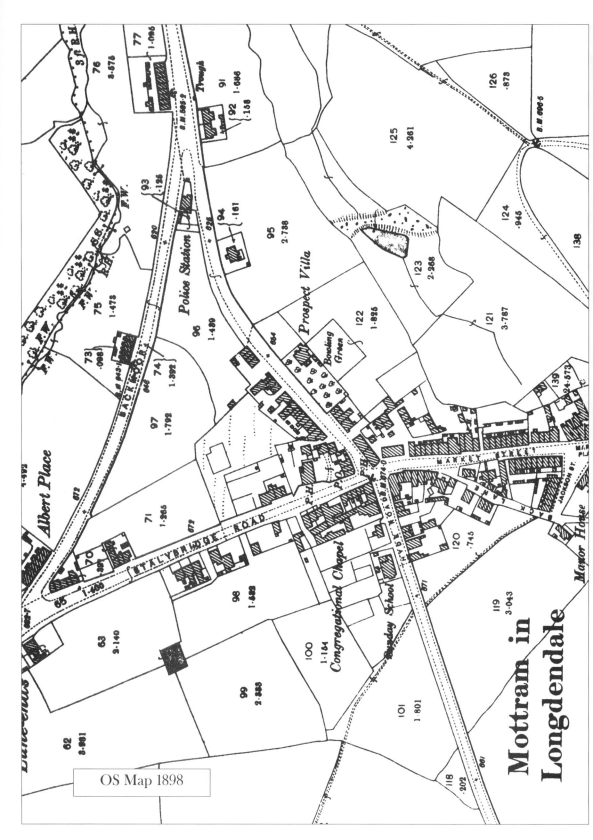

OS Map 1898

Mottram in Longendale

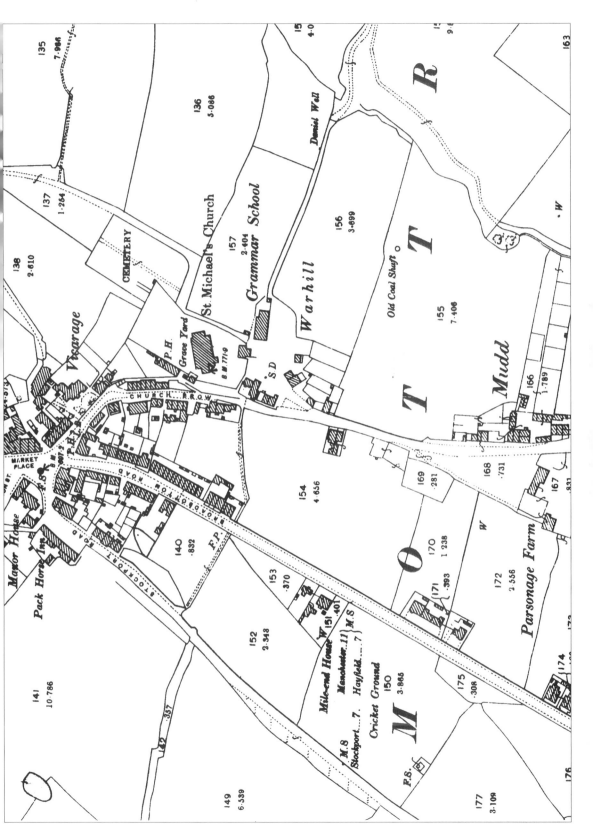

The arrival at Broadbottom Station of John Chapman Esq. of Hill End house. He was newly made High Sheriff
of Cheshire, and was demonstrating his faith in the new railway of which he was a director.

The Cotton Famine: operatives waiting for their breakfast in Mr Chapman's courtyard,
at Hill End House, Mottram, December 20th 1862

The Junction Inn with Miss Eyres' grocers shop opposite.

Looking from the Junction Inn, along
Stalybridge Road.

Dion parading the disgraced Mottram Cracker at the top of Mottram Moor. There was
a warning by the roadside. it said 'To cyclists this hill is dangerous!'

Outside the Junction Inn. Left to right Mary, Arthur and Polly. George and Dion standing in front of Polly.

The Baumeesters come to stay.

George, Jane, Dion and Phyllis raring to go to take part in the Village Carnival.

Eight
FAMILY LIFE AT MOTTRAM

Family life for the Wadsworths continued harmoniously at the Junction Inn. Jane was taken each day to attend the Misses Amps and Shelton Ladies' school, called Primrose House School in Primrose Lane, Glossop. Mary took care of Phyllis, still too young for school.

Dion and George went on to Mottram Grammar school after attending the church school run by Mrs Hardy until they were eleven. On weekdays during term time lunch was provided by the Inn for twelve of the boys from the Grammar school. Several other boys stayed for lunch at the Headmaster's house, but whenever it was politely possible, the boys would find an excuse to join the others at the Junction because the meals were more interesting and generous. The boys usually had soup, a cut off the joint with vegetables followed by fruit tarts. Dion would often take back to school a piece of fruit pie for a hungry friend who had to stay at school.

Lunch was served to casual travellers and regular callers. Miss Farrand, of 'private means', lived in splendid isolation in a large Georgian house called Prospect House on Mottram Moor. Miss Farrand was over fond of wine and the Inn kept her well supplied. Polly often sent a meal down for the lady who tended to neglect to feed herself. Her maids seemed unconcerned and her cook liked an easy life.

The bars at the Junction Inn at lunch time were filled with baskets of freshly baked bread to be eaten with pieces of crumbly mouth watering Cheshire cheese accompanied by a dish of pickled onions.

Monday was 'washing day' when Mrs Dearnley would come to wash the clothes. She worked most of the day, refreshed by several bottles of stout, and returned the following day to help with the ironing. For her labours she received three shillings. For tea on wash day there were always mussels; these were shelled, seasoned and butter added. When mussels were not available then plaice or finnan haddock was served instead because every Monday 'Fish Sal' arrived in the village with a large basket of fish balanced upon her head. She could always be relied upon for plaice and kippers.

Every Wednesday Polly had a 'baking day' when she made her bread and pastry. A favourite dish on baking day, loved by the children, was made by Polly using left over pieces of bread dough. She rolled the pieces into small round balls and dropped them into a pan of boiling water to simmer for five minutes. The fluffy balls of dough were removed from the pan and they were put to drain. Polly would break open the top of each dough piece that was now puffed and swollen and into the space she would drop warmed golden syrup.

Polly made most of her pastry with homemade lard from the pigs. Sometimes chicken fat or dripping was used for pastry especially for pigeon and rabbit pies, which were especially delicious. She often made 'raised or standing pies', with 'hot water pastry' at the end of the week so that they could be 'cut at' during the weekend. There was always lots of homemade bread. Arthur was so keen on his wife's bread that whenever he went off on holiday he would take a couple of her loaves with him!

Food played a great part in their lives. The young family were taught good table manners. Following Arthur's example the brothers always brought their sisters' chairs to the table and saw them seated. Each child had its own initialled napkin ring made of bone and a napkin. If any child ever put an elbow on the table for a second, the flat side of the carving knife would descend upon their knuckles with the reproof, *'all joints upon the table carved'*, from their Mother. The family waited to begin eating until everyone had been served. Arthur was always served first and Polly had to learn to tolerate his habit of cutting off a piece of his meat and putting it into the nearest mouth waiting for his or her meal.

No arguments were allowed at the table so generally family meals were happy affairs apart from the frustration felt when the children had to put their quarrels on hold for the duration of the meal. Breakfast was always a cooked meal, especially in the winter time when the surrounding countryside was bleak, raw and very cold. The biting winds made music all through the winter months in the village at the top of Mottram Moor. Breakfast began with porridge, pinhead oatmeal that had been 'steeped' overnight near the stove. In the morning it was cooked slowly in a double saucepan to avoid the oatmeal 'catching'. This same oatmeal was sometimes concocted into a delicious baked pudding on busy winter lunchtimes. Usually home cured bacon and eggs or bacon and kidney followed. Sometimes it would be finnan haddock poached in milk. Kippers were a firm favourite with the family and were sent regularly from friends in the Isle of Man as well as from Fish Sal.

Toast was rarely eaten unless it was with turkey dripping and essence sprinkled with pepper after Christmas. Whoever made the toast sat on a buffet in front of a red glowing fire with a plate of cut bread on one side of them and another plate on the other side of them to receive the hot toast. The bread was speared on a long extending metal 'toasting fork' held in front of the fire.

Lunch always started with soup, followed by a cut off a roast joint. Pork was never served unless there was an 'R' in the month. Pork flesh was suspect in any other month it was believed. Arthur disliked lamb so that was never served. Chicken was in good supply so it was served regularly boiled and roasted and not as a treat as was the custom in other households.

In winter when fresh vegetables were in short supply, diced carrots and turnips or swede were cooked together and mashed with butter and sprinkled with pepper. Cabbage was cooked and drained thoroughly into a colander. A small plate was placed on the drained cabbage until all the excess water was squeezed away. It was then glazed with butter and sprinkled with pepper.

Carrot 'hash' was served up if there were elaborate meals being prepared for a function at the Inn. Equal quantities of minced meat, minced carrots, minced onion and a small amount of minced swede were seasoned, thickened and cooked slowly in a casserole dish. The 'hash' was served with creamed mashed potatoes.

Puddings were mostly in the form of pies and open tarts using gooseberries, apples, blackberries, mincemeat or marmalade. Wimberries, collected on the moors by local people, were sometimes made into sponge puddings. When the pudding was turned out onto a plate and the deep purple juice trickled down the sides of the pudding, this was the cue for a family murmuring of a verse from the hymn, 'All things bright and beautiful'; it went, *'The purple headed mountain, the river running by, the sunset and the morning that brightens up the sky'*.

Tea was considered a light meal. They had dishes like minced kidney, cooked and thickened and served on toast with a poached egg on top. Undercut steak was fried and also accompanied with a poached egg. Pickled herrings were a family favourite. They were filleted, scaled and seasoned and smeared with butter before they were rolled and simmered in diluted vinegar.

Frequently there was sherry trifle, sometimes made with layers of fatless sponge cake spread with raspberry jam and well soaked in sherry. It was covered in a thick layer of egg custard and topped with a layer of thick cream. It was invariably decorated with half glacé cherries and blanched almonds. Fruit was sometimes used in a trifle and placed in layers between the sponge, soaked in fruit juice and white wine. The custard and cream layers were added and the top decorated with mauve and pink sugared violets.

When in season, strawberries or rasperries were crushed with icing sugar and made up as a layered sponge cake and covered with thick cream. 'Sweet loaves' were always there to fill up an odd corner during the evening. If they were very hungry butter was spread over a thick slice of Madeira or seed cake.

Fresh fruit was kept in plentiful supply, especially apples, pears and oranges, then four for a penny. Pomegranates were popular and once armed with a small spoon to pick out the juicy seeds it would occupy a child for some while. Grapefruit was never seen in the shops but occasionally one was on display at a local bazaar or garden fête when a wealthy patron might send one down from the 'Hall' to be displayed as 'a new fruit from America'. It was not until the Americans joined the First World War that American soldiers made them a popular fruit here.

Tomatoes were treated with caution as it was rumoured that they may cause cancer. It took several years for these fruits to find public favour.

During the game season there were plenty of grouse and pheasants to prepare, not a job for the faint hearted. Guinea fowls were a popular dish with the family, especially served cold. Polly would 'cure' some of the pretty feathers to trim her hats. A pie was made of the giblets from any of these fowl.

A delicacy reserved for Polly were 'squabs', baby pigeons out of the nest. She would place them with a little liquid and seasoning in a small white earthenware jar and cook them slowly in the oven.

Arthur would sometimes take Dion with him on a 'sparrow hunt'. He had to shoot many sparrows for Polly to make into a pie for herself. Country sparrows were a very difficult shot. Snipe, a small bird with a long beak, about the size of a swallow, was also a difficult shot. They were found over marsh land. Polly would prepare them by looping their beaks into their necks. They were tied with string and hung to cook before the fire in a 'Dutch oven'. Snipe had a unique straight gut and a sign that they were cooked to perfection was when their innards fell out!

Another of her specialities was 'jugged hare'. The leveret was skinned, blooded, jointed and placed in a large earthenware jug along with an onion stuck with a few cloves. Then the jug was filled with port wine and cooked slowly in the oven until tender. To complete the dish, just before serving a small amount of the hare's blood was added to the juices.

The only meal of the week that Polly did not prepare was Sunday breakfast when Arthur performed his only culinary task of the week. First he would cook all the bacon until it was crisp and brown using the Dutch oven. Next he would break the eggs into the pan one by one and baste each egg until it was a cloudy pink. The plates of bacon and egg were served to the family in turn as they sat around the kitchen table, each child patiently awaiting the proffered plate from their father. Arthur cooked his own egg last, before finally sitting down with his family. The rule was that the first person served would wait before leaving the table until the last person had finished. Arthur always enjoyed a leisurely Sunday breakfast.

Polly attended evensong at Mottram church where her two sons were in the choir. All the children were encouraged musically. Jane attended Mr Cottrell in Glossop for piano lessons. She adored the piano and with his encouragment she passed many Royal College of Music examinations.

Phyllis was gifted with a fine singing voice and later she was sent to a good 'Singing Madam' for lessons in Glossop. They were also taught by their mother to love and care for the many books that they had in their home. Both parents encouraged the children to take part in sports. As soon as they were able the children attended swimming lessons in the grand new swimming baths in Howard Park in Glossop.

Arthur was not the disciplinarian in the family; this he left to Polly. He never raised his hand to his family. He would gently bid his children to him using an old English expression "come your way". Arthur would over-indulge in alcohol from time to time and gradually the family came to know the signs. He had a fine tenor voice which he rarely used but when he had been drinking he would stand by the piano and instruct Jane to accompany him as he sang *'I'm a fine old English gentleman'* with feeling. Phyllis, who had a sweet clear singing voice, would sing *'When Irish Eyes are Smiling'* until tears filled his eyes and he was ready to retire to recuperate.

He relied upon his adorable Polly to organise his family life as well as most of his business life whilst he relaxed and enjoyed himself being 'mine host'. Unfortunately, Polly could see to the incoming bills but she had no control on the money coming in. The catering bills were paid to Arthur who could be irresponsible in the spending of it. He bought her jewellery and encouraged her to dress well. In fact he would not be seen out with anyone who was not well dressed. He once refused to walk with his sister-in-law, Sarah, at a family funeral. Sarah, small and plump, was unable to buy a suitable black outfit and had to borrow a long ill-fitting coat from a friend. Arthur took one look at her and walked behind her in the procession into church.

Hats were the one thing that Polly and Arthur disagreed about. On one occasion Polly came home from shopping at Bon Marché in Glossop, wearing a new hat that she was very pleased with. Arthur's reaction was to remove the hat pins from his wife's hat, and toss it into the fire. The next time he went into Manchester he visited the fashionable Marshall and Snelgroves in St Anne's Square and purchased a hat that met with his approval.

He would frequently spoil his wife and family in ways that caused Polly much irritation because of the money he spent. She occasionally sulked and he would be desolate until his sentence was over. To his friends and relations he was a cheery straightforward man's man and he enjoyed the warm regard of all who knew him.

After several years of making a great deal of money Arthur was inclined to live like a lord. He was a member of the Cheshire Yeomanry under the command of Col. Sidebottom JP VD, a prominent member of the local Conservative Association, and in 1904 he became a member of Mottram in Longdendale Urban District Council. He was a member of Mottram Masonic Lodge 320 and later a founder member of the Hadfield Lodge.

Arthur was a keen sportsman. He was an excellent shot, and a member of the local shooting club winning many handsome prizes. He was an early member of Glossop Golf Club and went on to win several Captain's prizes. He took a keen interest in cricket and Derbyshire cricketer, Harry Bagshaw, was a good friend. He kept the George and Dragon Inn on the Moors at Woodhead. (Harry's grave in Eyam, Derbyshire, has carved upon it a cricket bat and ball, stumps and bails flying and the umpire's upturned finger)

Later on in life, as widows, Polly and the irrepressible Mrs Bagshaw became firm friends. She used Polly as her mentor for correct table etiquette and culinary advice for many years, running her extensive public house in a grand manner which made her as well known as her late husband.

Arthur was President of the Mottram Central Football Team when they competed in the Glossop and District Football League and won the Partington Cup in the season 1899/1900. Not to be outdone, Polly became Captain of Mottram Women's Cricket Club.

Polly kept her head high and worked hard hoping that some of the money coming in would be saved for a rainy day - but their extended families were fooled by the display of fine clothes and jewellery and their affluent way of life.

Mary looked after Phyllis and was competent enough to take her off her Mother's busy hands. She had an odd assortment of interests that the small girl had to partake in. Mottram had its own brass band and Mary was a 'groupie'. Brass bands had an hypnotic affect upon her like the sound of the pipe has upon the snake of a snake charmer. As soon as the first dulcet tones were heard in the distance Mary would gather up Phyllis and bundle her into her pram, ready to file in after the band as it went past. Off they would go, following the band until it disappeared into the bandroom. Sometimes they would be out for hours if the band visited another village. Hail, rain or shine she was always there. At first these lengthy absences alarmed Polly but she eventually accepted this idiosyncrasy of Mary's.

During the early years of the 20th century many of the villages had a brass band who on the slightest pretext would don their uniforms and march around the village playing for the people's delight. Christmas, New Year, Easter, Whitsuntide and the 'Wakes Week' were their official appearances, but nearly every weekend they would be heard playing somewhere. Some of the village bands became prize bands competing annually at Belle Vue Pleasure Grounds near Manchester.

On the Sunday of Whitsuntide, from 8 am onwards, the band appeared in the centre of the village to play in silvery tones 'Hail Smiling Morn' and other requests before moving elsewhere in the village. Householders gave generously when a collection was held although it was mainly the local magnates who financed these bands.

Mottram Team Which Won Cup 35 Years Ago

The above is the Mottram team which won the Glossop and District Football League in 1899-1900. The figure on the left in civilian attire is the President, Mr. A. Wadsworth, and the thirteen players are: G. Atherton (goal); Moses Fernly, John Salmon, W. Barlow (full backs); F. Kenyon, W. Andrew, G. Slack (killed in the war), E. Rhodes (half-backs); P. K. Marsland, G. Lloyd, A. Marsland, T. Kershaw and A. Bevan (forwards.

This team lost the first match 11—0 against Glossop St. James's, at Glossop, and then went through without defeat, and had only one more goal scored against them—truly a wonderful record by a fast and clever side. We believe no other football cup has been won by a Mottram team since 1900 until Friday last, when Mottram Central won the Partington Cup at Glossop, a report of which match and the presentation of the Cup by Mr. S. T. Ashton, will be found in our inside pages.

Mottram team photographed with Arthur in their hour of glory 1899/1900.

Polly, centre, Captain of Mottram Ladies Cricket team.

A more macabre pastime Mary participated in was the viewing of the dead. Throughout the social classes the Edwardians believed in burying their dead in as much style as their money - or their insurance company - would allow. It was a mark of respect to the deceased for people to call at the house of mourning and ask to see 'them'. Mary, using Phyllis as an excuse for a walk in her pram, would wait until the Inn was quiet then slip out, and holding Phyllis by the hand she would invite herself in to view the body. No one thought it unusual for small children to be taken to view the dead, so no one thought to mention the frequency of Mary's visits. But eventually Polly was told of this fascinating hobby of Mary's, and an alarmed Polly dealt with Mary so severely that Phyllis never again accompanied Mary on these visits.

Polly had an occasional holiday when she would take her son George with her to an hotel in Llandudno. But Arthur did not like her being away - he was proud of her immaculate style and her independent spirit, but he developed an unreasonable jealousy. He was not happy until she returned home.

Arthur would take holidays. If he was going to behave himself and not drink, he would take his eldest son George with him to the Isle of Man, a place that he loved dearly. If he was intent upon a drinking spree he would take his unfortunate second son Dion with him to Blackpool for a few days.

The Wadsworth children grew up thinking the world was a safe place, especially if you were born in England. They used the village streets as a playground. When the horse and waggon crawled up Mottram Moor with the weekly supply for the Co-operative stores, the driver would stop, climb down and lift up the two small girls sat in the middle of the road on three-legged stools, complete with their stool, and then place each little girl down safely upon the pavement. He would climb back upon his waggon and proceed on his way, his ears ringing with their shrieks of laughter. It became a weekly entertainment for them all.

Dion and George would go off to fish in a local pond. They would rush home with their catch, and bound up the stairs into the living quarters to deposit it into the large fish tank in the window overlooking Hyde Road.

When the children became bored they would visit Mary in the kitchen and as she was usually busy she would send them off into the village upon 'errands'. Phyllis was despatched to the gentle Miss Eyre in her grocery shop for a pint of 'pigeon milk', and her friend was sent to her uncle, Mr Wittingslow for the book *The Life of Adam's Grandfather*. Dion was sent to Mr Goddard at the sweet shop for 'a two penn'orth of kick me' or 't' counter drops'. Usually the trouble that ensued would occupy the bewildered children for a considerable time.

During the Summer months there was great fun to be had playing in the old horse cab in the orchard that Arthur had bought for his children. Here they drove to the far ends of the earth and Mottram was quite forgotten. Phyllis developed a real love for the old cab and would nestle down on its horsehair seat to dream away. On one occasion she had fallen into a deep sleep and when she failed to answer all the calls and the summer evening began to fade, anxiety mounted in the house. A search party was formed for the blue-eyed flaxen-haired child and soon the search extended to the surrounding fields. Anxiety turned to fear as the men returned having found no trace of Phyllis. Suddenly they spotted a small figure standing in the doorway sleepily rubbing her eyes and looking most puzzled at the emotional reception. No one had thought to look into the old horse cab.

When the snow came, as it often did during the long bleak winters upon the moor, the children were forced to play indoors. Mary, in order to be rid of them for a moment, would ask them if they wanted to make real ice-cream. To the whoops of delight they would muffle themselves up and run out onto the white carpeted bowling green. Here each child armed with a spoon and a cup would fill their cup with snow and race back into the kitchen for a spoonful of sugar to mix with the snow. This they were told was real ice-cream - eat it all up. Sometimes Mary would pop the cups into the oven for a moment and then they had an iced drink.

Playing indoors could be dangerous. Once Polly and Arthur had gone into Manchester for the day and the three eldest children were left in Mrs Dearnley's charge. Left to their own device, a chase around the many rooms soon developed between George, Dion and Jane. Finally they all met in the Tap room and there were great shrieks of laughter, only to turn to fear as Jane's long flowing dress caught the flickering flames of the Tap room fire. Fanned by the draught as she ran in terror around the room, the flames began to get a hold. George stood rooted to the spot with horror but Dion leapt into action. He pushed Jane down onto the hearth rug and rolled her up in it, beating out the offending flames - most courageous for a young boy. Mrs Dearnley entered the Tap room on hearing the cries of terror just as Dion rolled Jane in the hearth rug. At once she presumed that in horseplay that had gone on, it was Dion who had pushed Jane into the fire. Probably feeling guilty herself for failing to supervise the children she turned her wrath upon Dion. After the excitment died down and she was assured that Jane had only minor burns and a severe fright, Mrs Dearnley dealt with Dion by banishing him to his room and giving him a beating. It was only when his parents returned that the truth came out and justice was restored - a little late as far as Dion was concerned.

Being a village community there was an awareness between people of their varying circumstances. Every Sunday Polly sent one of the boys with dinner for two old people living in a nearby cottage. She would always send them pancakes on Shrove Tuesday. Within their means people helped each other, not in the condescending manner of some of the 'Toffs' but in a down-to-earth, no nonsense, quiet way. Most neighbours 'pitched in' to help if there was sickness or hardship in a home. Usually it was children that were sent with gifts of food to less fortunate households, concealed from view in a wickerbasket covered with a lace edged embroidered cloth. Sunday afternoons seemed to be the time when the man of the house retired for a doze. The wife would bustle round her kitchen and prepare a basket. Into the basket would go a couple of brews of tea screwed into a ball of greaseproof paper, a small pot of lemon curd with a couple of homemade buttered 'barm cakes', perhaps a few slices of meat or ham and a jar of pickles. Over the contents went the cloth and a child was summoned to deliver the basket to the nearby cottage. They were given strict instructions that they were not to go into the cottage but sit outside on the step. Here the child sat until the basket was relieved of its treasure. When the basket was returned, the child would hurry home.

One miserly man who was earning the princely sum of a £1 a week with only a wife and one child to keep, watched every penny his wife spent. He decreed that she made her own

Arthur on his precious Bowling Green with his pupils, sons George and Dion.

Polly with George, Dion and Baby Jane at the Junction.

bread and never bought more than four 'balm cakes' a week, and she was allowed to bake only one sweet cake a week. But this did not stop his wife from waiting until he left on Sundays to ring the bells at church. As soon as he was out of sight, mother and daughter would dash into the kitchen and prepare a couple of food baskets for their less fortunate neighbours and quickly dispatch them. When the husband returned he was oblivious of the feverish activity while he had been bidding village souls to come to church to pray to the Almighty.

Mrs Bevan was a great asset to Polly for she would help out when needed at the Junction Inn. It was a Godsend to Mrs Bevan as well, for on these occasions she never went home empty handed. Before she started to help out at the Inn, feeding her family had been a difficult task. She lived with her husband and five surviving children in a small cottage *'down the Moor'*. Her husband was a foreman colour mixer at the Print Works in Hollingworth and she had to be a good manager - her husband would proudly boast that his wife could make a meal out of a 'dish clout'. Every day the farmer delivered a quart of milk - they did not buy pasteurised because it was thought to spoil the taste and it was more expensive - and most days she managed to obtain her family a 'taste' of meat. At the butcher's she would buy 'bits' from a large bowl into which the butcher put the scraps from trimming the meat and sold off cheaply towards the end of the day. Mr Aquila Patchett, the butcher, would sit behind the horseshoe-shaped wooden display counter of his shop front with a large fly swatter, to swat the flies and bluebottles that gathered on the scraps.

She baked daily for her family and they ate lots of root vegetables. A treat for the family was buttermilk. Apples and oranges were shared between the five children, sometimes half each, sometimes a quarter. Eggs were a special treat - the cooking was seldom enriched with them - and one egg was divided between two children. At Easter and birthdays each child had a whole egg. Mrs Bevan would run into debt before letting her children go hungry and when food was scarce she would try to make the food as interesting as possible for the children gathered round the table.

Despite these privations the Bevans were a happy devoted family. The only real shortage within the family were clothes. These would be passed down to each child in turn. The eldest boy joined the Army at 17 and the youngest girl went into service at the tender age of 11 years. The remaining three children stayed in the village.

Early in 1909 Polly began to feel most unwell. She consulted Dr Awburn who lived with his sister at the Manor House in Mottram. She was shocked to be told by Dr Awburn that she was pregnant. George was 15 years, Dion 13, Jane was 11, Phyllis was 6 years old. Although Polly was aware that most of their financial survival depended upon her she felt that she could no longer cope with the treadmill of running the catering at the Junction Inn. Despite all her industry she feared that little money had been saved and for a short period of time most of the fight in her nature deserted her. It was time for things to change.

Polly with Mottram Cracker.

H.E. Tonge

Florence Studio
Stalybridge
94 High St.

Miss Farrand of Prospect House, Mottram Moor, shakes hands with Polly for the photograph.

Arthur, Mine Host,
and below, in his younger days, in the Cheshire Yeomanry.

Polly and Arthur, dressed for the occasion, Polly wearing a hat that Arthur approved of.

Arthur in his Masonic Regalia.

MOTTRAM-IN-LONGDENDALE
Urban District Council.

TO THE RATEPAYERS OF MOTTRAM.

LADIES AND GENTLEMEN,

It is now three years since you elected me to be one of your representatives upon the Urban District Council, and during that period it has been my constant endeavour to fulfil the duties in that spirit of progress combining **Efficiency with Economy** which was set forth in the address I issued in March, 1904.

I have constantly pressed for the **abolition of the antiquated sytem of lighting** he roads with oil lamps, and a successful start has been made on Broadbottom Road, through obtaining the laying of gas mains thereon, and the Hyde Road is to have gas extenced to the boundary without further delay. The Gas Company has also undertaken to lay mains along the road to the Matley boundary in the Roe Cross Cutting. Another extension of gas improvement I have successfully advocated has been the **early morning lighting** which is of considerable benefit to the workers, especially women and children during the winter months.

I am also strongly in favour of **cheaper gas and cheaper water** for the householders.

The district still lacks efficient means of communication for travelling to Railway and Tram Termini I have done my utmost to obtain extensions and facilities to connect these together, and I am not without hope that the early future may see some development in this matter which I should in every possible way endeavour to assist and promote.

Highways and Sanitary matters have received my attention, and if you re-elect me I shall continue to give to these subjects, which are of constantly increasing importance, my very best consideration, as I think Mottram should have such modern improvemen's as would tend to make it as attractive a locality as possible, to induce more permanent residents to settle here.

I remain, Yours obediently,

ARTHUR WADSWORTH.

Remember on Saturday, March 23, 1907, at the National School, Mottram, between 12 noon and 8 p.m.

VOTE STRAIGHT AND EARLY FOR

LOMAS & WADSWORTH
AND NO MONOPCLY OR LUXURIES.

Printed and Published by ELI CLIFFE, Roe Cross, Mottram ; Works—Stalybridge and Dukinfield.

Arthur's Election Address.

Church Brow, Mottram.

Mottram village children, George 7th from the left.

Mottram Moor.

The Precious Mary.

Jane and Phyllis seated behind the bus driver. George is third from left in the road.

Mottram Moor. The Junction Inn is at the very bottom of this steep street.

Mottram bellringers.

Phyllis, Arthur, Polly, Dion, Jane; George sitting on rug at front.

Howard Park, Glossop, showing the Baths and the Woods' Memorial at the entrance to the park.

Hadfield Mill.

Nine
RETURN TO HADFIELD

The upshot of it all was that Polly and Arthur moved from Mottram in 1909 to take over the busy Commercial Inn in Hadfield, and the faithful Mary went with them. The Inn was known locally as the 'Red Lamp' because of the red glow from the lamp hung over the outside front door. Arthur was to be the tenant.

It was Arthur's native village, and the mill village where they had first met many years before when Polly escaped from Sheffield to join her three siblings who had already moved to the Glossop area, away from their prosperous, very busy father and stepmother, with their second family.

Polly was proud of her mother's family who had married into the Heathcote's of Chesterfield, descendants of Mompesson of Eyam. Her mother Jane had been banished by the family when she eloped with a farmer's son from Oxton, Nottinghamshire. They had met when he played the violin for hymn singing in her church. Because of this Polly never knew her mother's family until her mother had been dead for many years and an Aunt Heathcote of Park House, Newbold, near Chesterfield, made herself known to her father, to enquire about her sister's children.

Polly's heart was heavy with the move; she had no wish to return to Hadfield and the close scrutiny of the Wadsworth clan who all seemed to have prospered by their industry. But Polly kept her head high, and fortunately for her she was expected to withdraw into her quarters because of what people in whispers called 'her condition'.

The Commercial Inn was a smaller establishment than the Junction and it did little or no catering for it was at the wrong end of the village, away from the railway station, to catch any passing trade. It was situated at the bottom of Station Road by the crossroads that led directly to the Waterside Mills complex and the steep walk up to the village of Tintwistle. It faced Bankbottom, the road that led up to the hamlet of Broscroft and the way to the beauty of the wooded, Longdendale Valley reservoirs.

The road to the left of the Inn ran by the Conservative Club and St Charles Catholic church and school. It passed Samuel Chadwick's Sheet Metals, tin and coppersmith's establishment, at the end of Woolley Bridge Road. Eventually the road led to Woolley Bridge and on to Hollingworth and the steep pull up the Moor to Mottram.

Bankbottom housed the Irish Catholic colony. Many of the Irishmen called 'July Barbers' arrived every June to help with the hay making, but some of them had married Hadfield girls and settled in the cottages in Bankbottom. The Anglo/Irish families were looked down upon by the rest of the village population - if your family had an Irish name and lived in Bankbottom, you were on the very bottom rung of the social ladder!

Polly found that one of the few compensations of living in Hadfield was the excellent train service to her native Sheffield, and to Manchester and Glossop. There was also a good tram service from the top of Station Road that ran to Old Glossop.

With the money left over from running the Junction Inn at Mottram, Arthur bought two shops and a small cottage with an orchard, at the bottom of Bank Street, near the Inn. He used the orchard for his livestock. One shop was a sweets and tobacconist's, the other a bakery and confectioner's shop next door. Next to that was the cottage he bought for Mary who was to marry David Winterbottom, a Hadfield boy.

The Commercial was a double-fronted, three storey, stone building with a large cobbled courtyard at the rear. Its trade was based upon the Waterside Mills complex and people coming and going to Tintwistle, or along the road that led to Woolley Bridge and the Bleach Works in Hollingworth. It catered for the area around and as part of this Arthur provided weekly entertainment for his customers. He organised strictly adults only wagonette trips to the Old Glossop Wakes, held over a weekend in September. The trip cost two pence. For an extra penny on their return, they could go into a room set aside in the Commercial and partake of a glass of wine and a fancy bun.

On November 19th 1909, a third daughter was born to Polly and Arthur. In a fit of insanity they called her Wilhelmina Wanda Wibberley. The first name after the Queen of the Netherlands, the middle one from a book that Polly had been reading before the birth, and Wibberley because it was Polly's maiden name. Warrington had also been proposed, after John and Hannah at the Workhouse who were to be Godparents. It was seriously debated but wisely dropped just before the christening. Fortunately her name was soon abbreviated to 'Mina'. The new baby took up a great deal of Polly's time.

Phyllis was the first in the family to suffer financially from the move from Mottram. The two boys finished their education at the Grammar school in Mottram and Jane continued to attend her private school in Glossop. But it was decided that Phyllis would attend the church school in the village and not join Jane at the private school.

She was fast developing into a tomboy, and Polly consoled herself that she was unlikely to benefit from private education as Jane had done! Phyllis lacked the aloof, ladylike ways that Jane had acquired, and she tended to react against it by appearing more devil-may-care. She did not fare particularly well at school but she made a lifelong friend of Georgina Mitchell and seemed happy.

Jane spent a great deal of time with her friend from school, Dorothy Malkin, whose father was a wealthy corn merchant and Mayor of Glossop. The Malkins were friends of Hannah and John Warrington at Glossop Workhouse, and the family lived in splendid isolation at Moorside, a large house with seven bedrooms above Old Glossop.

Dorothy rarely visited Hadfield and Jane felt better staying with the Malkins; they sympathised silently with Jane now that her family were reduced to less prestigious circumstances in Hadfield. Jane preferred to be away from her annoying younger sister, Phyllis; since the move the sisters had to share a bedroom, and their mother was always busy with the new baby, Mina. The Malkins ate no better than the Wadsworths - they had the same breakfasts that Jane had at home, with Clara Malkin doing most of the cooking, although she had two maids to help her. Lunchtimes were the same as at home, with a joint or the universally popular dish for all classes, meat and potato pie. It was usually finished with a pudding and a cup of tea. Their evening meal was 'high tea' that was finished with tea or coffee, and cheese and biscuits were available for supper.

The Malkins did not have wine with their meals when they dined just as family but there was always whisky, burgundy and port in decanters on the sideboard and anyone who called in the evening unexpectedly was always offered a drink. Sundays, if there were no guests, consisted of breakfast, church, lunch, and evensong followed by a cold meat supper, for it was the maids' half-day off.

Jane always shared Dorothy's bedroom, and whenever the Malkins gave one of their supper parties, Jane and Dorothy were allowed to look down as the guests arrived, dressed in their finery.

When Dion finished school his parents decided that they could not spare him to go away from home to train to be a waiter at the Midland Hotel in Manchester, for he would have to be resident at the hotel. Dion, a tall dark haired boy, wanted no other profession so he decided to work for his father at the Commercial, much to Polly's pleasure, for despite his youth he was a hard and reliable worker.

Dion would rise at 5 am to make the coffee ready to open the Commercial doors for 5.45 am for callers going to work. A small rum and coffee was 2d, a large one 3d. He took little time off during the day and none in the evenings, for at night the Commercial was a very busy house. The singing room, and the other rooms, were always crowded. Dion and his brother George were expected to get straight back to work in the Inn when they returned from Tintwistle Church on Sundays.

Dion did not bother to negotiate for a wage or even weekly spending money. If he went anywhere Polly would give him some pocket money. George escaped most of the duties in the Inn, and continued with his job in a solicitor's office in Hyde.

Tintwistle Church had a thriving youth centre. The Rev. John Fairhurst was most popular with the young people in the area. Dion, George and their cousin Len Ford all attended Tintwistle Christ Church. George was a talented footballer and played for Tintwistle Church Club. George and Len Ford were both in the winning team that won the Hooley Hill and District Championship in 1911 and brought the first football cup to the village. George did not get home early from matches but when he did he was expected to help because Saturday nights were always busy ones. The three boys were all members of the 'Young Mens' Class' at Sunday school. Len later helped to form a Boy Scout group and coach the Tintwistle Harriers.

Like his father before him, George joined the Territorials, 6th Volunteer Cheshire Regiment (D Company TF). Dion did not because he could not be spared from the business.

All the children were expected to help, apart from Mina. One day they were given the task of peeling a sack of potatoes. Jane had just had her long brown hair washed by Mary, and was sitting in the kitchen, drying her hair, and refusing to help. To make matters worse she said, *"When I grow up I shall have a maid to do all that!"* and raised her hand in a dismissive gesture towards the two buckets of peeled potatoes.

George and Dion, usually slow to anger, each picked up their bucket of potatoes and emptied the contents over Jane's head! Her screams quickly brought the adults to the scene and an apology to Jane from her two brothers was demanded by Polly. Mary was none-too-pleased for she had the task of washing Jane's long hair once more.

Arthur was involved in founding the new Masonic Lodge and the consecration of the Lodge of Hadfield (3584) was arranged for March 12th 1912. There were 14 founder members; one 'Brother' was Frederick Bismark Fisher, Arthur's brother-in-law, married to his sister Jane. Polly and Jane were firm friends and their children were good companions.

The inaugural banquet was held upon the 20th March 1912 and attended by 200 prominent Freemasons from all parts of the High Peak and North Cheshire. Tickets were 15 shillings each. Polly was persuaded to return to catering for this one important occasion when the large Club room on the first floor of the Commercial was converted into a dining room for two days. Her menu included:

Soup: Hare and Oxtail
Fish: Cod with Oyster Sauce
Entré: Kidneys and Mushrooms
Relèves: Roast Ribs of Beef, Roast Mutton, Boiled Mutton
Removes: Roast Turkey, Sausages, Roast Ducklings, Roast and Boiled Chicken
Entremets: Hadfield Pudding 3584 Sauce, Tarts, Jellies, Custards
Cheese: Cheshire and Gorgonzola
Dessert: Fruits Nuts

The Musical Programme was shared by Bro G.W. Crowther, Solo Alto at Manchester Cathedral, who sang *If I built the world for you* and *The Sweetest Flower.* There were duets, *Watchman, what of the night?* and *Tenor and Baritone*, and recitals by Bro Sidney Spencer of the new Lodge.

When Mina was two years old she developed tuberculosis of the spine. All that was prescribable in those days was lots of rest, sunshine and fresh air. But no expense was spared to seek a cure. Polly and Arthur were willing to try anything; Dr Awburn from Mottram called regularly, and as Mina grew, a masseur came every week. Family life now revolved around the little invalid who to her credit was always bright and cheerful. Whenever the sun came out she was wheeled into the small orchard in her spinal carriage.

From time to time she was encased in plaster and eventually she wore a heavy leather, padded spinal jacket to support her spine. Mina only grew to be 4 ft 5 inches as an adult.

Tuberculosis in any form was not discussed in those days. There was a great deal of fear and ignorance, and also prejudice, about the disease. People talked dramatically of 'galloping consumption'. It became almost shameful to admit to having any form of the disease. It was easier to blame Mina's condition on the fall that she had suffered when she was two years old.

The Nuns at the nearby St Charles Convent agreed to undertake her education as she was such a bright child. She was trundled daily along the road to St Charles school in her long wicker spinal carriage.

Polly tried to see that her other children were not neglected, and despite her busy lifestyle, she regularly had some of her brother James's children over from Sheffield to stay. James and his wife, Annie, sent their children by train. The four young Wibberleys were locked into their railway compartment in Sheffield by the guard and he kept an eye upon them until he put them off at Hadfield Station.

Arthur would preside over the excited gathering of the clan on the station platform and then escort them all back to the Commercial in a crocodile fashion.

The girls, Phyllis and Jane with their cousins Kit and Annie, slept together on a large

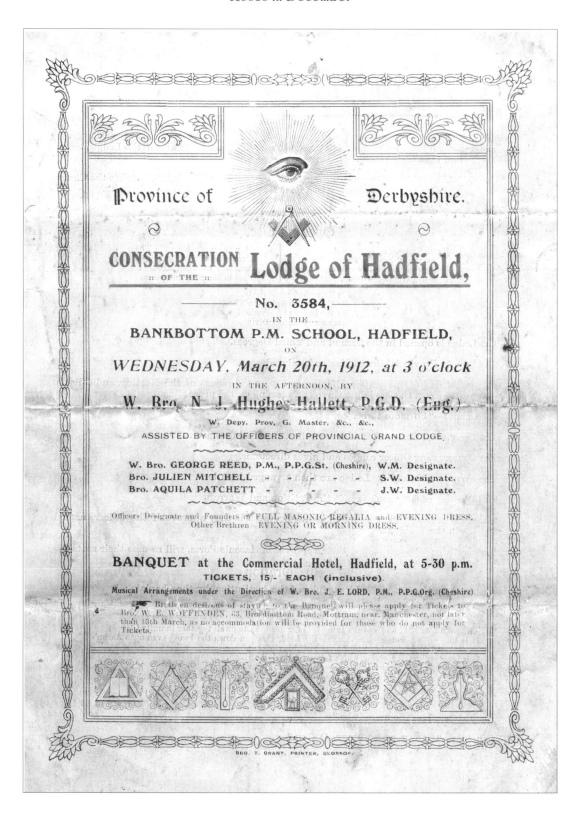

Province of Derbyshire.

CONSECRATION
:: OF THE ::
Lodge of Hadfield,

No. 3584,

...IN THE...

BANKBOTTOM P.M. SCHOOL, HADFIELD,

ON

WEDNESDAY, March 20th, 1912, at 3 o'clock

IN THE AFTERNOON, BY

W. Bro. N. J. Hughes-Hallett, P.G.D. (Eng.)

W. Depy. Prov. G. Master, &c., &c.,

ASSISTED BY THE OFFICERS OF PROVINCIAL GRAND LODGE.

W. Bro. GEORGE REED, P.M., P.P.G.St. (Cheshire), W.M. Designate.
Bro. JULIEN MITCHELL - - - - - S.W. Designate.
Bro. AQUILA PATCHETT - - - - - J.W. Designate.

Officers Designate and Founders in FULL MASONIC REGALIA and EVENING DRESS.
Other Brethren—EVENING OR MORNING DRESS.

BANQUET at the Commercial Hotel, Hadfield, at 5-30 p.m.
TICKETS, 15/- EACH (inclusive).

Musical Arrangements under the Direction of W. Bro. J. E. LORD, P.M., P.P.G.Org. (Cheshire)

Brethren desirous of staying to the Banquet will please apply for Tickets to Bro. W. E. WOFFENDEN, 63, Broadbottom Road, Mottram, near, Manchester, not later than 13th March, as no accommodation will be provided for those who do not apply for Tickets.

BRO. T. GRANT, PRINTER, GLOSSOP.

The four cousins, sat at the front on the floor, after a swimming lesson at Woods Baths in Howard Park. From left Jane, Phyllis, Ada and Beattie Fisher.

Annie, Phyllis and Kit, grown up.

feather bed in one attic back bedroom, while the four boy cousins slept together like sardines in another top front bedroom. Fortunately the constant fun and games and gales of laughter from the eight cousins on the top storey were insulated by the noise of the inn rooms below.

The girls would lie in bed in the early morning and listen to the rattle of the brew cans against the men's belt buckles, and the deafening clatter of clogs on the sets of the main street at the back of the inn, as the workers walked to the Waterside Mills. The cousins were equally fascinated to watch the millworkers returning home after their shift, with fragments of cotton fibres clinging to their hair and clothes.

Kit Wibberley was a shy girl, but even more of a tomboy than Phyllis, while Annie Wibberley was a gentle soul who formed a close friendship with Phyllis. The children were free to roam the countryside around, and they would walk over to Glossop Workhouse to visit Aunt Hannah and Uncle John and play on the swings and see-saw in the pauper childrens' playground.

Other times they would go to Woods Baths in Howard Park, Glossop, for a swimming lesson. Jane and Phyllis detested their swimming lessons, even when they were with their cousins Beattie, Ada, Kit and Annie. It seemed to Phyllis that all the female instructor ever did was tie a long rope around your waist and pull you along the entire length of the bath. This barbaric treatment put her off for life and she never did learn to swim, even though some of the others did. The only thing she remembered enjoying was the giggling session they all had walking 'over the top' and down North Road into Howard Park - and more than ever on their way back home.

If the children became bored anything could happen, especially if the two tomboys got together. On one occasion Kit and Phyllis went across the road to the orchard where Arthur kept his poultry, just after a killing session, and acquired two severed hen heads. Kit carefully dried them and placed them into small cardboard boxes. Then they brought them back to the Commercial and persuaded Annie to 'gift wrap' them in pretty paper and coloured string. Phyllis waited until the road was clear and crept out into the yard, opened the big gate and placed one of the dainty packages upon the pavement. She dashed back inside and the three girls raced up the stairs to the back bedroom with a good view of the package lying on the pavement. They fell about with laughter as passers by looked at the dainty package, until someone furtively popped the promising-looking package into their coat or their basket, and hurried on. Phyllis popped the second package in the street for a repeat performance.

The girls would walk over to visit their Uncle Bill and Aunt Sarah who owned the Organ Inn in Hollingworth. This inn had an interesting story. In 1819 Mottram Church decided to buy a new organ and opened a subscription list. The money raised was more than enough to buy the organ and the surplus was used to buy land in Hollingsworth where they built a row of cottages. The fund from the rents was administered by the Organ Trust and paid to maintain the organ and the salary of the organist. It was set up in 1824 and in the same year the inn was built and named after the trust. Adjacent to the inn, to the right, was a three-storey building with a large gateway which led through to a yard with a brewhouse and stables. In the 1870s it housed a ginger beer manufactory.

Sarah and Bill Wibberley were fun loving characters. Sarah was a great favourite with the children for she was small and cuddly and wore a bun on the top of her head which would

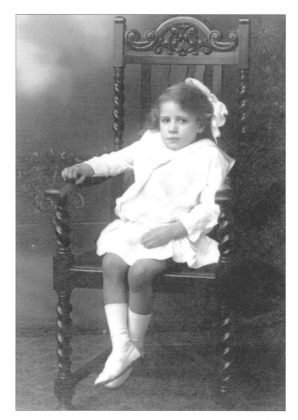

Wilhelmina Wanda Wibberley Wadsworth, known as Mina.

Mollie Dearnley.

slip in all directions as she scuttled about laughing. She would lead the children down the long garden at the back of the inn and find a poor unsuspecting frog. She would take a stick, touch the poor frog's rear and make it hop towards the safety of the well in the garden.

Once Sarah got her leg stuck as she sat on the brick wall of the well. There she sat with her plump jelly-like body, shaking and wobbling with mirth, and the children were completely unable to help her, they were laughing so much. Uncle Bill arrived on the scene, lifted his wife into his arms, deposited her into a big wooden wheelbarrow and wheeled her back up the garden, followed by the giggling children. Back in the kitchen it was refreshments all round for the thirsty group.

In 1913 Arthur 'had words' with the Brewery and the family moved out of the Commercial Inn across the road to their sweets and tobacconist shop at the bottom of Bank Street. Arthur had bought the shop with a view to Jane running it after she finished school. Dion found a job in a gentlemen's outfitters in Glossop. The bakery next door was rented to Harry and Esther Chadwick who became the best maker of vanilla buns in the village. They were good friends to Polly and Arthur, and Polly had the use of their upstairs rooms until the Chadwicks moved in and bought the shop from Arthur.

The adjoining cottage was occupied by Mary and her new husband, David, who worked in one of the many village butcher's shops. Now they lived next-door-but-one Mary still did a great deal for Polly, despite having a son, 'young David', and later a daughter, 'young Mary'.

Once more Polly had to adjust her life, this time to running a shop. She was by now 44 and Arthur was 46. The Commercial Inn was taken over by the Dearnley family who had come from Manchester where Mr Dearnley's family had a large double-fronted high class grocer's shop in Deansgate. The story was that Mr Dearnley had married the family's cook and it had alienated him from the family. Their eldest son John was away at school, and they had a daughter Mollie and a small son, Arthur.

For a period of time Mollie joined Phyllis at the local elementary school in Hadfield - which did nothing to help Phyllis's concentration. Mollie was frequently banished for bad behaviour from the classroom into the cloakroom where she invariably proceeded to dress up in the teacher's hat and coat! She would dance about the cloakroom and catch the attention of Phyllis and her friend Georgina Mitchell who sat near the cloakroom window - so they had a ring-side seat. They were horrified by Mollie's daring antics.

Eventually Mollie was sent to Manchester High School for Girls - until she was expelled for having tea with a senior boy from Manchester Grammar School in the State Café, a fashionable restaurant in Piccadilly.

Mollie and Phyllis began a firm friendship that was to endure until Mollie married and went to live in South America. Phyllis also adored Mollie's small brother Arthur which was just as well because the girls looked after him a great deal. Arthur was a sweet natured child but had one great fear and that was a bearded old drunkard called Zachariah, who was forever being thrown out of the Commercial and banned. Zachariah lived in a mens' lodging house in Station Road. When he was really drunk the young people would go to considerable lengths to avoid him, terrified that he might make a lurch at them. When young Arthur Dearnley was put to bed at night he would always say his prayers, and then add *"I lub eberybody in de world, 'cept Zachawiah!"*

The one bane for Phyllis's visits to the Commercial was the donkey that Mr Dearnley allowed to roam in the large backyard of the inn. She would tentatively open the small back door and hurl herself across the yard to the safety of the back porch. Mr Dearnley was puzzled at Phyllis's behaviour and her unwillingness to use the backyard. When she admitted that she was afraid of his frisky donkey Mr Dearnley retorted, *"You're afraid; afraid of Jesus Christ's pal?"*

Arthur still reared poultry in the small orchard at the back of their garden and Dion had been taught early on how to do the killing. Tuesday afternoon was his half day off, but before he went off to indulge in his passion for sports, he was expected to clean out the hen cotes. If he tried to postpone this smelly job, he was brought back to do the task.

Arthur decided to sell eggs and poultry ready for the oven, but in a much bigger way than before. He would tour the nearby moors where he bought eggs and poultry cheaply from the isolated farms. He planned to sell them with his own from the shop. At weekends he would take George, Dion and Phyllis with him collecting eggs from farms around Holme Moss and Hey Edge. They booked a return ticket on the railway to Dunford Bridge, alighted at Crowden and set off walking over Holme Moss. The children humoured their fond father by going on these expeditions but thought it a drag, and more so as they filled up the egg baskets and staggered back over the moors to catch the train back to Hadfield.

A Moorland farm above Hadfield.

Fortunately their expeditions faded fast as Arthur thought up a far better way to gather his eggs. Polly's brother Bill, who owned the prosperous Organ Inn in Market Street, Hollingworth, had a pony and trap, so from now on Bill and Arthur did the egg collecting rounds. This was not always a good idea as the men would call upon their old friend Harry Bagshaw, the cricketer, and his wife at the George and Dragon Inn up on the moors near Woodhead. Of course they needed a respite from their labours - and the three men would over-indulge in liquid refreshment. On more than one occasion the pony brought Arthur and Bill back to Hadfield with the two men, drunk to the world, sitting happily in the boxes of smashed eggs. When Bill was asked how he could trust his pony to bring them back safely, he always answered, *"I'd trust him to drive me to bloody blue blazes and back".*

Sarah Wibberley tolerated her husband's occasional over-indulgence. One evening Sarah had retired early to her bed and lay quietly in their large brass-railed bedstead. Bill, who had consumed more than a wee drop, crept up the stairs into the bedroom hoping not to disturb her. As he felt his way along the rails at the foot of the bed Sarah's voice piped out, *"Are you playing the harp for me, Bill?"*

Despite the changes in their circumstances, Polly ran the business in her usual efficient manner, as well as caring for Mina, despite the minimal profits selling sweets. Arthur happily drifted from job to job, always optimistic. His drinking continued. If he was merely stepping out for a drink and male companionship he crossed the road to the Conservative Club. If he wished to drown his sorrows he would make for the Working Men's Club.

Arthur was cheerful and charming and enjoyed the love and affection of his family and friends. Polly always supported him although there was not really sufficient money for his busy social life. She remained calm and dignified throughout life's tribulations, and after Arthur's death at the age of 60, she had the complete devotion of all her children as she continued to battle *'to make ends meet'* and to care for Mina.

Hadfield Church School. Phyllis is third row, fifth from the left.

Polly with Mina in 1909.   Aunt Heathcote of Park House, Newbold, Chesterfield.

Jane with Dorothy Fielding.

Dion Wadsworth

1st Tintwistle Boy Scouts 1913. Len Ford, in charge, is centre picture. Dion Wadsworth is centre, back row.

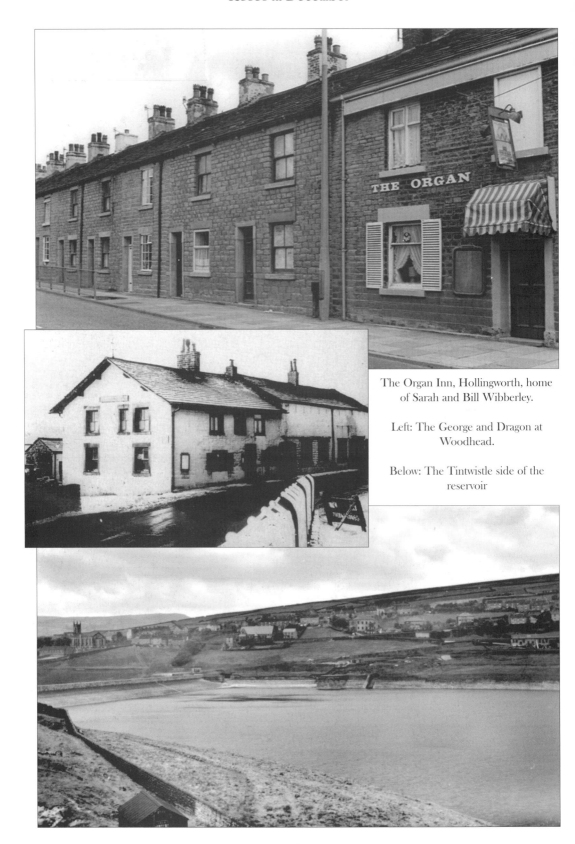

The Organ Inn, Hollingworth, home of Sarah and Bill Wibberley.

Left: The George and Dragon at Woodhead.

Below: The Tintwistle side of the reservoir

The last picture of all the Wadsworth family together in 1912.

Waiting for the Carnival to arrive, in New Road, Tintwistle.

The Champions, 1911.
Len Ford is seen on his haunches at the front; George is third row, 4th from right.

Territorial Camp.
George second row, 7th from left.